George Whitefield
TRUMPET OF
THE LORD

George Whitefield
TRUMPET OF THE LORD

Ruth Gordon Short

Review and Herald Publishing Association
Washington, D.C. 20012

Editor: Thomas A. Davis
Book Design: Alan Forquer

Printed in U.S.A.

ACKNOWLEDGMENTS
The material in this book is drawn largely from the writings of the Reverend L. Tyerman: *The Life of the Rev. George Whitefield, B.A., of Pembroke College, Oxford* (London: Hodder and Stoughton, 1890. Two volumes); *The Life and Times of the Rev. John Wesley, M.D., Founder of the Methodists* (London: James Sangster and Company, 1876), and John Gillies, D.D., *Memoirs of Rev. George Whitefield* (New Haven: Whitmore and Buckingham and H. Mansfield, 1834).

Library of Congress Cataloging in Publication Data

Short, Ruth Gordon.
    George Whitefield, trumpet of the Lord.

    1. Whitefield, George, 1714-1770.   2. Evangelists—England—Biography.   3. Evangelists—United States—Biography.   I. Title.
BX9225.W4S54   269'.2'0924 [B]   79-15420

Contents

A Stage-struck Lad

The stage-struck boy would rather act than do anything else he could imagine, unless it were reading plays. He would stay home from school for days at a time in order to prepare himself for some amateur play in which he was to take part. Gifted with an excellent memory and a natural aptitude for elocution, he was also fortunate in having a teacher who insisted that the students learn to speak and write correctly. He was thus prepared for a life of public appearances—far different, however, from the sort he contemplated!

George Whitefield was born at Bell Inn, Gloucester, England, December 16, 1714. For the information we have about his childhood and youth, we are entirely dependent upon an autobiography he wrote when he was in his twenties. It is an artless and ingenuous account in which he was so eager to exalt God's grace that he may have overemphasized his own depravity. At any rate, he was repeatedly denounced by his opponents in afteryears for the candor with which he wrote his journal. Compared to Augustine's *Confessions,* however, it seems harmless enough.

George was the youngest of seven children. His father died when he was 2 years old, so his mother bestowed on him all the more care, determined that he should have every possible inducement to succeed.

However, George says that he was so brutish he hated instruction, and was addicted to lying, filthy talking, and foolish jesting. "Stealing from my mother," he writes, "I thought no theft at all, and used to make no scruple of taking money out of her pocket before she was up." Often he took the money to buy fruits and tarts to satisfy his "sensual appetite," but sometimes he gave the money to the poor. He also stole books from his friends, but, strangely enough, they were books of devotion. In later years he was happy to restore them fourfold.

During his turbulent adolescence he often felt the movings of the Spirit of God upon his heart sufficiently to persuade him that God loved him with an everlasting love, but not sufficiently to make him turn from his reckless habits. He longed to be free from the confinement of school, and when he was 15, managed to convince his mother that if he studied any more Latin it would unfit him for the life of a tradesman. He argued that, since she could not give him a university education anyway, he might as well forget the classics and stay at home to help her at the inn, which she owned.

From then on he did janitor work at the tavern, and also stood behind the bar at times dispensing drinks. When his mother turned the inn over to his older brother, George had such a disagreeable time trying to get along with his brother's wife that he decided to leave and go to live with another brother in Bristol. He said that by this means God was forcing him out of the public-house business and calling him from drawing wine for drunkards to drawing water out of the wells of salvation for the refreshment of His spiritual Israel.

In Bristol, the Lord gave George foretastes of His love, and filled him with such an insatiable hunger and thirst after righteousness that he was carried beyond himself. He wanted to spend every moment possible in devotions, and wrote his mother that he would never go into public employment again. "But in the midst of these illuminations," he tells us, "something surely whispered, 'This will not last.'"

And so it happened. For when he left Bristol, he left his devotions, also, and being without employment, allowed himself to become recklessly absorbed in the pursuit of pleasure. "Much of my time I spent in reading plays, and in sauntering from place to place. I was careful to adorn my body, but took little pains to deck and beautify my soul. Evil communications with my old schoolfellows soon corrupted my good manners. By seeing their evil practices, the sense of the Divine Presence I had vouchsafed unto me insensibly wore off my mind, and I at length fell into abominable secret sin, the dismal effects of which I have felt, and groaned under ever since."

But though George's love for God was fickle, God's love for him was felt to be eternal. One morning as George was reading a play to his sister, he said, "God intends something for me which we know not of. As I have been diligent in business, I believe many would gladly have me for an apprentice, but every way seems to be barred up, so that I think God will provide for me some way or other that we cannot apprehend."

About this time a young friend of theirs, at the time a student at Pembroke College, Oxford, dropped in to see them. He mentioned how he had paid his way through college working as a servant for other students. George's mother was so excited that she cried out, "This will do for my son," and gave herself no rest until she had made arrangements for him to go to Pembroke. But first he had to finish his preparatory training, and so reentered the school he had so joyfully left a couple of years earlier.

"Being resettled in school," he writes, "I spared no pains to go forward in my book. God was pleased to give me His blessing, and I learned much faster than I did before. But all this while I continued in secret sin; and, at length, got acquainted with such a set of debauched, abandoned, atheistical youths, that if God, by His free, unmerited, and especial grace, had not delivered me out of their hands, I should long since have sat in the scorner's chair, and made a mock at sin. By keeping company with them, my thoughts of religion grew more and more like theirs. I went to public service only to make sport and walk about. I took pleasure in their lewd conversation."

But as he was "running on in a full career to hell" God put in his heart such a distaste for his activities that he was enabled to break away from his "darling sin." Nevertheless, he became intoxicated two or three times and felt that he was once again back in the clutches of Satan.

Remorsefully, the 17-year-old lad resolved to prepare himself for the holy sacrament. "I began now to be more and more watchful over my thoughts, words, and actions. I kept the following Lent, fasting Wednesday and Friday, thirty-six hours together. My evenings, when I had done waiting upon my mother, were generally spent in acts of devotion, . . . and I constantly went to public worship twice a day. Being now upper-boy, by God's help I made some reformation amongst my schoolfellows. I was very diligent in reading and learning the classics, and in studying my Greek Testament, but was not yet convinced of the absolute unlawfulness of playing at cards, and of reading and seeing plays, though I began to have some scruples about it."

A little later he dreamed that he was to see God on Mount Sinai but was afraid to meet Him. He told the dream to a woman, who commented, "George, this is a call from God."

His mother, however, reacted differently to the powerful impressions that came to him. "One night," he writes, "as I was going on an errand for my mother, an unaccountable, but very strong impression was made upon my heart that I should preach quickly. When I came home, I innocently told my mother what had befallen me; but she, like Joseph's parents, when he told them his dream, turned short upon me, crying out, 'What does the boy mean? Prithee hold thy tongue,' or something to that purpose."

For a whole year he continued praying, fasting frequently, receiving the sacrament monthly, and attending church constantly. His brother told him all this would not last when he once got to Oxford, and so George prayed all the harder that God would make him persevering.

When he reached his eighteenth birthday, it was judged time to send him to the university. He tells us that for this, God had "sweetly prepared" his way: "The friends before applied to recommended me to the master of Pembroke College. Another friend took up ten pounds upon bond, which I have since repaid, to defray the first expense of entering; and the master, contrary to all expectations, admitted the servitor immediately."

Under these auspicious circumstances, George Whitefield commenced his college career.

The Bible Bigot

In 1732 when Whitefield entered Oxford as a freshman student, that university was the last place in the world where one might expect to find any spirituality. Infidelity was rampant, and religion was scorned. The church had reverted to formalism, and it was considered rather rude and uncultured, even by professing Christians, to talk about such a thing as the new birth. There was no offense in carousing; there was much offense in the cross. It was all right to discuss Plato, but not in good taste to talk of Paul. A man was up-to-date if he read Rousseau, but a bit old-fashioned if he was familiar with Romans.

In such an atmosphere Whitefield was indeed regarded as an odd fellow. Rather than join in the rioting of his roommates, he sat alone in his study, where it was so cold his limbs were numb. For more than a year he longed for the companionship of those young students derisively called Methodists, but was too timid to make himself known to them. However, the opportunity came one day, and it marked a joyful occasion for him. A poor woman in the workhouse had attempted suicide. Whitefield thought someone like Charles Wesley ought to visit her, and so George commissioned an old woman to go to Charles to suggest this. At the same time he instructed her not to reveal who had sent her.

Happily, this request was not obeyed, and when Charles learned who had sent this message, he invited Whitefield to have breakfast with him the next morning. This was the beginning of a warmly affectionate, lifelong friendship between the two young men.

Charles lent his fellow student several books, among which was one entitled *The Life of God in the Soul of Man*. "At my first reading it," wrote Whitefield, "I wondered what the author meant by saying, 'That some falsely placed religion in going to church, doing hurt to no one, being constant in the duties of the closet, and now and then reaching out their hands to give alms to their poor neighbours.' 'Alas!' thought I, 'if this be not true religion, what is?' God soon showed me; for in reading a few lines further, that 'true religion was union of the soul with God, and Christ formed within us,' a ray of Divine light was instantaneously darted in upon my soul, and from that moment, but not till then, did I know that I must be a new creature."

It is interesting to observe that Whitefield, like thousands of others, first tried to save himself by his own good works, before learning that by grace we are saved through faith, that our salvation is a gift of God that is impossible for us to earn, that the task of making us good is done by the Holy Spirit working in us "to will and to do of his [God's] good pleasure," and that only as we yield ourselves to His will without reservation can He accomplish the saving of our souls.

Like every earnest seeker to whom this marvelous revelation comes, Whitefield was so elated that he wanted to proclaim it to the whole world. There was still a veil before his eyes, and he understood only "in part"; but imperfect though his knowledge was, he wrote letters to his relatives, "telling them there was such a thing as the new birth." He seemed to them as one that mocked;

they thought he was out of his mind.

In fact, Whitefield was never to know the joy of having spiritual fellowship with his mother and sister. Charles wrote to him about them when George was visiting in America: "You will expect some account of your own household. But what shall I say concerning them? I must either deceive or grieve you; but you have a right to the simple truth. Your mother continues dead in sin, yet well affected toward us. Your sister (God help her! God convert her!) is far, very far, from the kingdom of heaven. She has forsaken the word, and servants, and ministers of Christ, put herself out of the bands, and is the worst enemy they have. . . . I know not what to do with her or for her, and had long since given her up had she not been the sister of my friend."

Whitefield now began to associate more intimately with the group of young men mockingly called the Holy Club, the Bible Bigots, the Bible Moths, or, more frequently, the Methodists, because they followed methodical rules and regulations designed to improve their spirituality. "I now began, like them, to live by rule," wrote Whitefield, "and to pick up the very fragments of my time, that not a moment of it might be lost. Whether I ate or drank, or whatsoever I did, I endeavoured to do all to the glory of God."

At first it was hard for Whitefield to go to bed and get up at a stated time, but this soon grew profitable and delightful. He gave about one hour a day to charitable works, such as visiting the sick and the prisoners, and reading to the poor. Twice a week he fasted.

The new life surging through him altered not only his habits but his tastes. "The course of my studies I soon entirely changed," he says. "Whereas, before I was busied in studying the dry sciences, and books that went no farther than the surface, I now resolved to read only such as entered into the heart of religion, and which led me directly into an experimental knowledge of Jesus Christ, and Him crucified. . . . The book of the Divine laws was seldom out of my hands; I meditated therein day and night; and ever since that, God has made my way signally prosperous, and given me abundant success.''

The first effect of living his new life was that he increased in favor with God and man. His company was much sought after, and his services for part-time work were much in demand. But soon he began to experience the truth of the statement that all who will live godly in Christ Jesus will suffer persecution. The master of the college frequently chided him for visiting the poor, and threatened to expel him if he ever did so again. His relatives were so alarmed over the change that had taken place in him that they thought him insane. Some of his fellow students showed their contempt by throwing dirt at him, and those for whom he worked refused to pay him. A couple of his dearest friends, too timid to be seen with him, forsook him entirely.

All this was an excellent preparation for the lifework that lay ahead of him, for he learned how to endure hardness as a good soldier of Jesus Christ.

At this time he was also besieged with many satanic temptations that almost overwhelmed him. A horrible fearfulness and dread swept over his heart; darkness enshrouded him, and he felt a strange weight upon him. "All power of meditating, or even thinking, was taken from me," he writes. "My memory quite failed me. My whole soul was barren and dry, and I could fancy myself to be like nothing so much as a man locked up in iron armour. Whenever I kneeled down, I felt great heavings in my body, and have often prayed under the weight of them till the sweat came through me." So much did the devil trouble him that for weeks he never slept more than three hours at a time. Whitefield was convinced that Satan had as real power over his body as he once had over Job's.

Such a period of darkness and horror is not unusual in the lives of men who have been chosen for a great work in the Lord's vineyard. "An horror of great darkness" fell upon Abraham (Gen. 15:12) before God made His great covenant with him. Jacob went through a time of trouble before his glorious deliverance from the wrath of Esau (chap. 32:24-26), and David must have gone through an experience similar to Whitefield's, for he says in Psalm 143: "The enemy hath persecuted my soul; he hath smitten my life down to the ground; he hath made me to dwell in darkness, as those that have been long dead. Therefore is my spirit overwhelmed within me; my heart within me is desolate. I remember the days of old; I meditate on all thy works; I muse on the work of thy hands. Hear me speedily, O Lord: my spirit faileth: hide not thy face from me, lest I be like unto them that go down into the pit."

During this period Whitefield's mind was assailed with "proud hellish thoughts" that distracted his soul. "But God made Satan drive out Satan," he writes, "for these thoughts and suggestions created such a self-abhorrence within me, that I never ceased wrestling with God till He blessed me with a victory over them. Self-love, self-will, pride, and envy, so buffeted me in their turns, that I was resolved either to die or conquer. I wanted to see sin as it was, but feared, at the same time, lest the sight of it should terrify me to death."

So artfully did Satan continue to work on him that he began to go into fanaticism, supposing that the spirit that prompted such attitudes was good and not evil. He carried self-denial to extremes, depriving himself of wholesome food, and neglecting his personal appearance. He spent days refusing to speak to anyone.

He could not concentrate enough to write a required theme, and felt that it would be good for him to confess this fact publicly in order that he might suffer for his Master's sake. The confession naturally resulted in the professor's thinking he had gone out of his mind.

George spent long hours outdoors in prayer, even when it was stormy, and consequently suffered much from the cold. He was driven to give up all his religious friends. This distressed him, but he was determined to do it for Christ's sake.

Whitefield's changed attitude soon came to the attention of Charles Wesley, who visited him to find out what was the trouble. Charles turned him over to his brother John, who helped to straighten him out. John advised him to take up the external forms of his Christian experience again, but not to depend upon them for salvation. "From time to time," wrote Whitefield, "he gave me directions as my various and pitiable state required; and, at length, by his excellent advice and management of me, under God, I was delivered from those wiles of Satan. Praise the Lord, O my soul, and all that is within me praise His Holy Name!"

This period of darkness and struggle had lasted about a year, and Whitefield emerged from it thin and so ill that he was under the care of a physician for weeks. But "God was pleased," he writes, "to remove the heavy load, to enable me to lay hold on His dear Son by a living faith, and, by giving me the spirit of adoption, to seal me, as I humbly hope, even to the day of everlasting redemption. But oh! with what joy—joy unspeakable— even joy that was full of, and big with glory, was my soul filled, when the weight of sin went off, and an abiding sense of the pardoning love of God, and a full assurance of faith broke in upon my disconsolate soul!''

Whitefield now began to read the Bible on his knees. For a time he laid aside all other books and devoted his studies entirely to the Scriptures. ''I got more true knowledge from reading the Book of God in one month, than I could *ever* have acquired from *all* the writings of men,'' he testified.

But although Whitefield received such comfort with his knowledge of the new birth, he was not yet perfectly enlightened on the great doctrine of justification by faith. Wesley himself had been no help to him on this, for he himself had not yet had his heartwarming experience. The young Bible Bigots at Oxford had all been legalists to begin with, and came in varied ways to a knowledge of the fact that the just shall live by *faith*.

''About this time God was pleased to enlighten my soul, and bring me into the knowledge of His free grace, and the necessity of being justified in His sight by *faith only,''* writes Whitefield. ''This was more extraordinary, because my friends at Oxford had rather inclined to the mystic divinity; and one of them, a dear servant of the Lord, lately confessed he did not like me so well at Oxford, as the rest of his brethren, because I held justification by faith *only.* And yet, he observed, I had most success. But, blessed be God! most of us have now been taught this doctrine of Christ, and, I hope, shall be willing to die in the defence of it. It is the good old doctrine of the Church of England. It is what the holy martyrs in Queen Mary's time sealed with their blood, and which I pray God, if need be, that I and my brethren may seal with ours.''

At the age of 21, Whitefield was admitted to holy orders in the Church of England. Of this solemn experience in his youth he said, ''I can call heaven and earth to witness, that when the bishop laid his hand upon me, I gave myself up to be a martyr for Him who hung upon the cross for me. Known unto Him are all future events and contingencies; I have thrown myself blindfold, and I trust, without reserve, into His Almighty hands.'' In that unreserved surrender lay the secret of Whitefield's marvelous power in soul winning.

His first sermon, which was on the new birth, was preached in the church of St. Mary de Crypt. A large congregation came to hear the young prelate who, despite his youth, preached with a sense of the divine presence and with authority. So strongly were his hearers affected that it was reported to the bishop that fifteen of his congregation had gone mad. The bishop replied, ''I hope the madness will not be forgotten before next Sunday.''

The Preaching of the "Prince of Preachers"

At one time when Whitefield was preaching in Edinburgh, a young Scotchman considered going to hear him preach, but put it off because he had heard so many criticisms of his fanaticism that he thought going would be a waste of time. However, he finally overcame his reluctance and went. He describes the effect the sermon had on him and the rest of the audience: "His text was Isaiah 33:13-17. The sermon exceeded all the sermons I ever heard. About the middle of it, I ventured to look up, and saw all the crowds around Mr. Whitefield bathed in tears. I listened with wonder and surprise, and had such a discovery of the plan of salvation as I had never known before. I was astonished at myself that I had listened to the idle tales concerning him, and thereby have been kept from hearing a burning and shining light, who had been instrumental in the hand of God for the good of so many thousands of souls. When I understood he was about to leave Edinburgh, I was distressed. I remembered more of that sermon than of all the sermons I had ever heard. I had a discovery of the unsearchable riches of the grace of God in Christ Jesus; as also of how a lost sinner was to come to God, and obtain mercy through the Redeemer. From this time, I was truly convinced of the necessity of a change of heart." This youth later became one of Wesley's itinerant preachers, faithfully sharing with others the blessings he had received through Mr. Whitefield's ministry.

Whitefield seldom had an unfruitful meeting. Few could withstand the movings of the Spirit, as the natural gifts of the preacher were fortified with His power. Whitefield was a born orator and actor, well equipped physically and intellectually to put across a message. His sonorous voice (which could be heard at times a mile away), his commanding presence, his cheerful countenance, his descriptive powers, his apt anecdotes—all were used by the Spirit to bring conviction to the hearts of his hearers.

Whitefield did not believe in reading his sermons or using notes. He wrote in his journal: "I think the ministers' preaching almost universally by notes is a certain mark they have in a great measure lost the old spirit of preaching. For, though all are not to be condemned who use notes, yet it is a sad symptom of the decay of vital religion, when reading sermons becomes fashionable where extempore preaching did once almost universally prevail. When the spirit of prayer began to be lost, then forms of prayer were invented; and I believe the same observation will hold good as to preaching."

After listening to Whitefield preach in a churchyard, one man wrote: "Under Mr. Whitefield's sermon, many, among the immense crowd that filled every part of the burial ground, were overcome with fainting. Some sobbed deeply; others wept silently, and a solemn concern appeared on the countenance of almost the whole assembly. When he came to impress the injunction in the text (Isaiah 51:1) his words seemed to cut like a sword, and several in the congregation burst out into the most piercing bitter cries. Mr. Whitefield, at this juncture, made a pause and then burst into a flood of tears. During this short interval, Mr. Madan and myself stood up, and requested the people to restrain themselves, as much as possible, from making any noise. Twice afterwards, we had to repeat the same counsel. O with what eloquence, energy, and melting tenderness, did Mr. Whitefield beseech sinners to be reconciled to God! When the sermon was ended, the people seemed chained to the ground."

Let it not be supposed that Whitefield carried his audience with him by preaching smooth things or prophesying deceits. Far from it! Said one of his hearers, "The politest, the most modish of our vices, the most fashionable of our entertainments, he struck at, regardless of everyone's presence but His in whose name he spoke."

Whitefield preached against theatergoing, cardplaying, horseracing, dancing, cockfighting, and all the popular diversions of the time. Speaking of the fires of hell, he said, "Now you are not weary of your diversions, nor heavy-laden with the sins with which they are accompanied; but then you will be weary of your punishments. Your cards and dice, your hawks and hounds, your bowls and pleasant sports, will then be over!" Again, the 24-year-old preacher spoke scathingly of "innocent" diversions: "They talk of innocent diversions and recreations. For my part, I know of no diversion but that of doing good."

Nor was it ear-tickling for the people to hear Whitefield preach on the total depravity of human nature: "O man! whosoever thou art that deniest the doctrine of original sin, if thy conscience be not seared as with a hot iron, tell me if thou dost not find thyself, by nature, to be a motley mixture of brute and devil? I know these terms will stir up the whole Pharisee in thy heart; but stop a little, and let us reason together. Dost thou not find that, by nature, thou art prone to pride? Otherwise, wherefore art thou now offended? Again, dost not thou find in thyself the seeds of malice, revenge, and all uncharitableness? And what are these but the very tempers of the devil? . . . Out of thy own heart, therefore, will I oblige thee to confess, what an inspired apostle has long since told us, that the whole world, by nature, lies in the wicked one, that is, the devil; and that we are no better than those whom St. Jude calls *brute beasts;* for we have tempers, by nature, that prove to a demonstration that we are altogether earthly, sensual, and devilish."

Such was Whitefield's language when he contemplated sin and the sinner. He believed that "secure sinners must hear the thundering of Mount Sinai, before we bring them to Mount Zion. They who never preach up the law, it is to be feared, are unskilful in delivering the glad tidings of the gospel. Every minister," said he, "should be a Boanerges, a son of thunder, as well as a Barnabas, a son of consolation." The truths he preached exalted the God of heaven and laid the pride of man in the dust.

Whitefield's sermons often consisted merely in telling familiar Bible stories, but with such wondrous pathos and power that one can scarcely read them without weeping. How much more profound must the effect have been on those who listened to him and felt the force of his Spirit-filled personality! One secret of his success was that he never ventured—to use his own language—to preach "an unknown Christ, *or to deal in the false commerce of unfelt truths.*"

When the chapel on Tottenham Court Road was built, it was dubbed by a neighboring doctor, "Whitefield's Soul Trap"—not a bad name, at that! His whole aim in life was to accomplish one purpose: to win souls for Christ. Said he, "Believe me, I am willing to go to prison or death *for* you; but I am not willing to go to heaven *without* you."

A hardheaded shipbuilder who went to hear White-field was asked what he thought of the preacher. "Think!" said he, "I never heard such a man in my life. I tell you, sir, every Sunday, when I go to church, I can build a ship from stem to stern, under the sermon; but, were it to save my soul, under Mr. Whitefield, I could not lay a single plank."

A distinguished man who met his own minister on his way home from a meeting of Whitefield's was asked disdainfully why he had gone to hear such a rambling preacher as Whitefield. "Sir," replied the gentleman, "when I hear you, I am planting trees all the time; but during the whole of Mr. Whitefield's sermon, I had no time for planting even one." This was not surprising, since Mr. Whitefield threw his whole soul into the task of preaching. "I preach till I sweat through and through," he said.

Most of his preaching was done outdoors, for even when he was permitted in the churches they could not contain the multitude. The number of people attending his sermons at various times was estimated at 10,000, 20,000, 30,000, 50,000, and even 80,000. It is surprising enough to visualize Whitefield standing in the rain preaching to 30,000 people; it is even more surprising to know that the people were willing to stand in the rain to listen. It must be borne in mind that his outdoor preaching was done in the winter, as well as in the summer, and that he was often half frozen while preaching. "On Tuesday at seven in the evening," he writes, "I preached in the open air to a great multitude. All was hushed and exceeding solemn. The stars shone very bright, and my hands and body were pierced with cold; but what are outward things, when the soul within is warmed with the love of God?" The "great multitude" must also have been pierced with the cold, but they considered it worth it to have the privilege of hearing Whitefield preach the Word.

One time nearly a thousand people on horseback came to hear him on a chilly November day, but "though it was cold, the congregation stood very patiently in the open air, and seemed in no hurry to return home after the discourses were ended." In Scotland people stayed in the fields until two o'clock in the morning, loathe to leave the scene of such blessedness.

The subject of his sermons was always apt. When he was preaching during the racing season, his text was "So run, that ye may obtain" (1 Cor. 9:24). It is said that Alexander Garden, a minister who was Whitefield's bitter opponent, preached against him from Acts 17:6: "These that have turned the world upside down are come hither also." Whitefield countered with a sermon enlarging on the words of 2 Timothy 4:14: "Alexander the coppersmith did me much evil: the Lord reward him according to his works."

If he was interrupted by a thunderstorm during his preaching, Whitefield was quick to make the most of it. A contemporary described his preaching on one such occasion: " 'See there!' said the impassioned evangelist, pointing to a flash of lightning, 'it is a glance from the angry eye of Jehovah! Hark!' continued he, raising his finger in a listening attitude, as the thunder broke in a tremendous crash, 'it was the voice of the Almighty as He passed by in His anger!'

"As the sound died away, Whitefield covered his face with his hands, and fell on his knees, apparently lost in prayer. The storm passed rapidly by, and the sun, bursting forth, threw across the heavens the magnificent arch of peace. Rising and pointing to it, the young preacher cried, 'Look upon the rainbow, and praise Him who made it. Very beautiful it is in the brightness thereof. It compasseth the heavens about with glory, and the hands of the Most High have bended it.'"

Preaching was for Whitefield a cure for any bodily infirmity he might have. He called preaching his *catholicon,* his cure-all. One time a physician, in accordance with the barbarous custom of the time, prescribed a perpetual blister for him. "But I have found perpetual preaching to be a better remedy," Whitefield remarked, fervently. "When this great catholicon fails, it is over with me."

Again, he writes, "I have been sick; but, blessed be God! I am better. Who knows but I may be strengthened to take a trip to Scotland. This itch after itinerating, I hope, will never be cured till we come to heaven."

Whitefield particularly loved preaching in the bracing outdoors; he felt that preaching indoors was apt to make him nervous. Often he spoke from one to four times a day, beginning at six or seven o'clock in the morning. Writing from London in the month of November, he said, "London already begins to disagree with my outward man, but the Lord's smiling upon my poor labours sweetens all. I have begun to preach at six in the morning. We have large congregations even then."

Like Wesley, Whitefield not only loved to preach in the early-morning hours but managed to get thousands to come out to hear him. When he visited Boston during the month of February, some laymen invited him to preach to them every morning at six. Of this experience he wrote: "Not expecting a very great auditory, I opened a lecture in one of the smallest meetinghouses, upon these words, 'And they came early in the morning to hear him.' How was I disappointed! Such great numbers flocked to hear, that I was obliged to make use of two of their largest places of worship, where, I believe, seldom less than two or three thousand hearers assembled. . . . It is impossible to describe the eagerness and punctuality of these early visitants. To see so many hundreds, of both sexes, neatly dressed, walking or riding so early along the streets to get food for their souls, has feasted my own heart. . . . Lecture, and family prayer, and breakfast, are over in many houses before the sun is suffered to come into the windows of others. . . . One morning the crowd was so great, that I was obliged to go in at the window. The high sheriff, who was most forward in persecuting good Mr. Davenport, accompanied me; and when he put his head into the window after me, the people were ready to cry out, 'Is Saul also among the prophets?' "

Luther insisted that the test of a good preacher was his ability to interest children, young people, and servants. He said, "When I preach, I sink myself deep down. I regard neither doctors nor magistrates, . . . but I have an eye to the multitude of young people, children, and servants, of whom are more than two thousand. I preach to those, directing myself to them that have need thereof. . . . An upright, godly, and true preacher should direct his preaching to the poor, simple sort of people, like a mother that stills her child. . . . In such sort should also preachers carry themselves, teaching and preaching plainly, that the simple and unlearned may conceive and comprehend, and retain what they say."

That Whitefield preached thus may be gathered from the experience of Benjamin Rhodes, who was 11 years old when he first heard the evangelist. Writing about it in later years, he said, "I went with my father to Birstall to hear Mr. Whitefield. I found my soul deeply affected under the word. At first, I had a kind of terror; but, before the sermon was ended, my heart was melted into tenderness, and sweetly drawn after God." Rhodes became one of the best of Wesley's itinerant preachers.

Thus, impelled by the Spirit, Whitefield preached in season and out of season, at sunrise and sunset, indoors and outdoors, in sunshine and shower, to young and to old, to aristocrats and servants, to learned and unlearned, never wearying, but ever refreshed by new enduements of the Spirit.

Popularity

In the course of his busy career Whitefield was "in journeyings often, in perils of water, in perils of robbers, . . . in perils in the city, in perils in the wilderness, in perils in the sea, in perils among false brethren; in weariness and painfulness, in watchings often" (2 Cor. 11:26, 27); but none of these things moved him from the steadfastness of his purpose to preach the gospel at home and abroad.

However, our adversary the devil knows well that such difficulties merely drive a true Christian closer to Christ, and at an early stage Satan tried on Whitefield the most subtle and insidious of all temptations: popularity. It is perhaps easier to be stoned for Christ than to stand for Him amid the plaudits of the multitude.

At the age of 21, Whitefield had already made friends with many aristocratic lords and ladies. One time, after visiting with Sir John Philips and perhaps feeling a bit exalted, he wrote, "God sent me something to ballast it; for, as I passed along the streets, many came out of their shops to see so young a person in a gown and cassock. One . . . cried out, 'There's a boy parson,' which served to mortify my pride, and put me also upon turning the apostolical exhortation into prayer, 'Let no man despise thy youth.'"

When he was only 22, he received a tremendous welcome at Bristol, where he preached for a month. At times almost as many were turned away from the church for lack of room as were admitted. Because he intended to depart for Georgia in the near future, his farewell was a sad one. Concerning this he wrote: "June 21st, I took my last farewell at Bristol; but when I came to tell them [the people], it might be, that they would *'see my face no more,'* high and low, young and old burst into such a flood of tears, as I had never seen before. Multitudes, after sermon, followed me home weeping; and, the next day, I was employed from seven in the morning till midnight, in talking and giving spiritual advice to awakened souls.

"About three the next morning, having thrown myself on the bed for an hour or two, I set out for Gloucester, because I heard that a great company on horseback, and in coaches, intended to see me out of town."

In London his popularity was just as great. "The tide of popularity now began to run very high," he wrote. "In a short time, I could no longer walk on foot as usual, but was constrained to go in a coach, from place to place, to avoid the hosannas of the multitude. They grew quite extravagant in their applauses; and, had it not been for my compassionate High Priest, popularity would have destroyed me. I used to plead with Him, to take me by the hand and lead me unhurt through this fiery furnace. He heard my request, and gave me to see the vanity of all commendations but His own."

Charles Wesley testified to the amazing popularity of his youthful friend. He wrote in his journal, "I met and turned back with Betty to hear Mr. Whitefield preach, not with the persuasive words of man's wisdom, but with the demonstration of the Spirit, and with power. The churches will not contain the multitudes that throng to hear him."

The people loved him so much that often, as he traveled from one place to another, as many as sixty or seventy on horseback would follow him. They seemed to wish that they might but touch the hem of his garment. The modern reader will perhaps be amused to learn that in the eighteenth century, as in the twentieth, people wanted to know what their heroes ate for breakfast. We learn that Whitefield "often appeared tired of popularity; and said, he almost envied the man who could take his choice of food at an eating-place, and pass unnoticed."

When Whitefield went to America, the temptations to spiritual pride were just as great. Writing of these to a friend, he said: "The innumerable temptations, that attend a popular life, sometimes make me think it would be best for me to withdraw. But then, I consider that He who delivered Daniel out of the den of lions, and the three children out of the fiery furnace, is able and willing to deliver me also out of the fiery furnace of popularity and applause, and from the fury of those, who, for preaching Christ and Him crucified, are my inveterate enemies. In His strength, therefore, and at His command, when His providence shall call, I will venture out again. As yet, my trials are nothing. Hereafter, a winnowing time may come; and then we shall see who is on the Lord's side, and who dare to confess Christ before men.

"I long to die unto myself, and to be alive unto God. Methinks, I would always be upon the wing; but, alas! I have a body of sin, which, at times, makes me cry out, 'Who shall deliver me?' I thank God, our Lord Jesus Christ will deliver. But I never expect entire freedom till I bow down my head, and give up the ghost. Every fresh employ, I find, brings with it fresh temptations. God always humbles before He exalts me. Sometimes I speak and write freely, at other times I am comparatively barren; one while on the mount, another while overshadowed with a cloud; but, blessed be God, at all times, at peace with Him, and assured that my sins are forgiven.''

In London again, the youth was given a welcome such as few had ever received. True, only one church was open to him, but that did not prevent his preaching in his open-air cathedral or his own wooden tabernacle. He wrote to a friend, ''It is too much for one man to be received as I have been by thousands. The thoughts of it lay me low, but I cannot get low enough. I would willingly sink into nothing before the blessed Jesus, my All in all.''

Apparently he had been a bit haughty at one time in his treatment of a certain minister, for he wrote to him: ''I have been much concerned since I saw you, lest I behaved not with that humility toward you, which is due from a babe to a father in Christ; but you know, reverend sir, how difficult it is to meet with success, and not be puffed up with it. If any such thing was discernible in my conduct, oh, pity me, and pray to the Lord to heal my pride. Alas! who can hope to be justified by his works? My preaching, praying, et cetera, are only *splendida peccata.** The blood of Christ, applied to my soul by living faith, is the only thing that can render them acceptable.''

The Lord has a marvelous system of checks and balances to keep His truly surrendered children from succumbing to that deadly sin: spiritual pride. Not alone through persecution and opposition, but through sickness and loss, through grief and deprivation, He lays man's glory in the dust. Thus He did with Paul, and a similar course He followed with Whitefield, lest he be exalted above measure.

---

* ''splendid sins''

Whitefield was often sick. Frequently he vomited blood after delivering a sermon. Sometimes he suffered from asthma. Repeatedly he expressed a desire to die. But he had learned in whatsoever state he was, therewith to be content. He knew how to be abased, and also how to abound, and it was well that he did, for the abasement followed hard on the heels of the abounding, as we shall see.

Cabbages and Cats

In Whitefield's great open-air cathedral in Moorfields, he learned the truth of Paul's statement: "All that will live godly in Christ Jesus shall suffer persecution" (2 Tim. 3:12). Moorfields was a strange place for him to choose for the setting up of his portable folding pulpit, but a great and effectual work was done there nonetheless. Whitefield described it as a place where Satan's children kept their annual rendezvous.

It was a large, spacious area of London where in the springtime all sorts of booths were erected for the use of mountebanks, players, puppeteers, boxers, gamesters, and exhibitors of wild beasts. With trumpeters and drummers summoning the people to their shows, it was a noisy, raucous atmosphere in which to attempt to preach the gospel.

Of his experience there one spring morning, Whitefield wrote: "With a heart bleeding with compassion for so many thousands led captive by the devil at his will, on Easter Monday, at six o'clock in the morning, attended by a large congregation of praying people, I ventured to lift up a standard amongst them, in the name of Jesus of Nazareth. Perhaps there were ten thousand waiting, not for me, but for Satan's instruments to amuse them. I was glad to find that, for once, I had, as it were, got the start of the devil. I mounted my field-pulpit, and almost all flocked immediately around it. I preached on these words, 'As Moses lifted up the serpent in the wilderness,' et cetera. They gazed, they listened, they wept. All was hushed and solemn; and I believe many felt themselves stung with deep conviction of their past sins.''

Encouraged by this experience, Whitefield ventured out again at noon, and said that the whole field seemed white for harvest—not, however, for the Redeemer's, but for Beelzebub's. About twenty or thirty thousand people filled the fairgrounds. He preached on the text "Great is Diana of the Ephesians," and drew so many people away from their amusements that the proprietors of the various booths were incensed. This led them to throw stones, dirt, rotten eggs, cabbages, and pieces of dead cats at the preacher. "My soul," wrote Whitefield, "was indeed among lions; but far the greater part of my congregation seemed to be turned into lambs."

Thus encouraged, he went there again at six o'clock in the evening to preach, and once more found thousands upon thousands engaged in their sports and amusements, but other thousands waiting to hear the gospel. A popular trumpeter performed on a large stage, but as soon as his listeners saw Whitefield, they left him and ran to the preacher, who later wrote that he was enabled to lift up his voice as a trumpet.

"At length," he adds, "they approached nearer, and the merry-andrew (who complained that they had taken many pounds less that day on account of my preaching) got upon a man's shoulders, and, advancing near the pulpit, attempted several times to strike me with a long, heavy whip but always, with the violence of his motion, tumbled down. Soon afterwards, they got a recruiting sergeant, with his drum, et cetera, to pass through the congregation. I gave the word of command, and ordered that way might be made for the king's officer. The ranks opened, while all marched quietly through, and then closed again. Finding these efforts to fail, a large body, on the opposite side of the field, assembled together, and, having got a large pole for their standard, advanced towards us with steady and formidable steps, till they came very near the skirts of our congregation.

"I saw, gave warning, and prayed to the Captain of our salvation for support and deliverance. He heard and answered; for, just as they approached us, with looks full of resentment, they quarreled among themselves, threw down their pole, and went their way, leaving, however, many of their company behind. I think, I continued in praying, preaching, and singing (for the noise, at times, was too great to preach), about three hours."

For three days Whitefield kept returning to renew his attack in Moorfields, and again was greeted with pelting, noise, and threatenings. One man climbed a tree and attempted to distract the attention of the people by indulging in obscene actions. Whitefield appealed to his hearers to believe that he spoke truly when he said that that man, left to himself, was half devil and half beast. Gaining their attention once more, the preacher concluded his sermon with a warm exhortation, and read many of the notes that were passed up to him from his listeners, in which they told of the work of God in their hearts.

Among the throngs who listened to Whitefield at Moorfields were several little boys and girls who sat around him as he preached, and passed the notes of the people to him. These children were often struck with the eggs, stones, and dead cats aimed at the preacher, but never once ran away or attempted to escape. Instead, they lifted their little weeping eyes to him and seemed to wish they could receive the blows for him.

All sorts of attempts were made on the evangelist's life. One time a man came to his house planning to assassinate him, but later confessed to his accomplices that, having been treated so kindly by the intended victim, he did not have the heart to touch him.

Murderous outrages were perpetrated against the Methodists as they attempted to congregate in their meetinghouses. The rioters would interrupt the services, fall upon the worshipers with blows and kicks, strip the women of their clothing, and drag them through mud and dirt. One poor woman at one of Whitefield's services was forced up into the gallery, where one of the mobsters attempted an outrage upon her. She screamed and struggled and freed herself by leaping over the gallery and making her escape. Although magistrates or officers of the law were implored to use their authority, none made any attempt to come to the assistance of the victims.

If the Methodists appeared on the streets, they were furiously pelted with stones, dirt, cabbage stumps, and anything else available—and all this in broad daylight. Preachers were imprisoned without any attempt to follow the due processes of law. One of them intended to preach in the playhouse, but then decided to hold his meeting in another place. Later he discovered he had made a fortunate change, for on the playhouse door was posted a notice, reading: "For the benefit of the mob. This evening will be acted at the theatre, Hell in an Uproar; or, the Furies Let Loose. The part of Beelzebub, by Mr. P.; Queen of Hell, by Mrs. L., et cetera."

It is sad to note that these outrages were committed by members of the Established Church, without any noticeable opposition or hindrance from the bishops. Many of the clergy were very bitter against Whitefield because they felt that his teachings tended to put them in an unfavorable light before the people.

There was a prolonged series of disturbances in Long Acre that resulted in a lengthy correspondence between Whitefield and Bishop Pearce. The bishop had prohibited Whitefield from preaching there, but Whitefield had been invited to preach, and if he wished, to use the liturgy of the Established Church in a duly licensed chapel of the Dissenters, and he intended to continue.

Writing to the bishop concerning the rioting, he said: "Drummers, soldiers, and many of the baser sort, have been hired by subscription. A copper furnace, bells, drums, clappers, marrow-bones, and cleavers, and such-like instruments of reformation, have been provided for them, and repeatedly have been used by them, from the moment I have begun preaching, to the end of my sermon.

"By these horrid noises, many women have been almost frightened to death; and mobbers have, thereby, been encouraged to come and riot at the chapel door during the time of divine service; and after it has been over, have insulted and abused me and the congregation. Not content with this, the chapel windows, while I have been preaching, have repeatedly been broken by large stones of almost a pound weight, which, though levelled at me, missed me, but sadly wounded some of my hearers. . . .

"I have only one favour to beg of your lordship. As the above-named gentlemen leaders of the mob are your lordship's parishioners, I request that you desire them, henceforward, to desist from such unchristian, such riotous, and dangerous proceedings.

"Whether, as a chaplain to a most worthy peeress, a presbyter of the Church of England, and a steady disinterested friend to our present happy constitution, I have not a right to ask such a favour, I leave to your lordship's mature deliberation."

It is not surprising that Whitefield's appeals to Bishop Pearce were so ineffective, for the wealthy bishop was a man whose fortune was built on the distillery business of his father and enhanced by his marriage to the daughter of another distiller.

During this period the Archbishop of Canterbury, stung as were others by Whitefield's insistence on emphasizing the doctrine of original sin, wrote to a friend, "The subjects of the Methodist preaching, you mention, are excellent in the hands of wise men, not enthusiasts. As to their notion that men are by nature devils, I can call it by no other name than wicked and blasphemous, and the highest reproach that man can throw upon his wise and good Creator."

If the Methodists were so cruelly persecuted by the members of their own church, the Church of England, it is no marvel that they were even more cruelly dealt with at the hands of the Roman Catholics in Ireland. In that troubled isle it took a great deal of courage for one to become known as a Methodist. In Dublin, the pulpit and benches of their chapel were burned in the streets. In Cork the persecution was particularly brutal.

With the connivance of the mayor and magistrates, "men and women were attacked with clubs and swords, and many were stabbed, gashed, slashed, stoned, and seriously wounded. Their houses were demolished, and their furniture and goods destroyed."

These people were members of various societies established by Wesley, but Whitefield interceded for them because of his connections with the nobility. Wrote he, "The dear souls have my constant prayers, and shall have my utmost endeavours to serve them. I count their sufferings my own." His efforts resulted in the presenting of a memorial to the king, a narrative of the persecution to the king's representative in Ireland, and to the secretary of state, the Duke of Newcastle, who expressed great resentment.

The persecutions in Ireland were much more severe than those in England, but it was doubtless easier to arouse sympathy among the authorities for the victims of the Irish Catholics than of the English Protestants. At any rate, after a long series of malevolent outrages in Cork, a semblance of tranquillity was restored there.

Several years later, when Whitefield itinerated in Ireland, he wrote from Dublin concerning the treatment he received from the mob after preaching in Wesley's meetinghouse: "Finding me unattended (for a soldier and four Methodist preachers, who came with me, had forsook me and fled), I was left to their mercy. Their mercy, as you may easily guess, was perfect cruelty. Vollies of hard stones came from all quarters, and every step I took, a fresh stone struck, and made me reel backwards and forwards, till I was almost breathless, and was covered all over with blood.

"My strong beaver hat served me, as it were, for a skullcap for a while; but, at last, that was knocked off, and my head left quite defenceless. I received many blows and wounds; one was particularly large near my temples. Providentially, a minister's house stood next door to the Green. With great difficulty I staggered to the door, which was kindly opened to, and shut upon me. Some of the mob, in the meantime, broke part of the boards of the pulpit into splinters, and beat and wounded my servant grievously in his head and arms, and then came and drove him from the door of the house where I had found a refuge. . . .

"At length, a carpenter, one of the friends who came in, offered me his wig and coat, that I might go off in disguise. I accepted of them, and put them on, but was soon ashamed of not trusting my Master to secure me in my proper habit, and threw them off in disdain. Immediately, deliverance came. A Methodist preacher, with two friends, brought a coach; I leaped into it, and rode, in gospel triumph, through the oaths, curses, and imprecations of whole streets of papists, unhurt.''

To another friend Whitefield later wrote, "The blows I received were like to send me where all partings would have been over. But, I find, *we are immortal till our work is done.''*

In America

I could do no more for a season, than whilst I was writing, now and then to turn my head, by way of reproof, to a lieutenant of the soldiers, who swore, as though he was born of a swearing constitution. Sometimes he would take the hint, return my nod, with a 'Doctor, I ask your pardon,' and then to his cards and swearing again."

Thus wrote Whitefield concerning the uncomfortable situation in which he found himself on his first voyage to America. The captain of the ship—which was full of soldiers—the officers of the regiment, and the surgeon made it clear to him that they looked upon him as an impostor. As if this were not sufficiently distressing, there was no way whereby he could escape from them for a little private prayer and study, for he had no place of retirement.

Part of the time Whitefield sat on the deck, reading Arnd's *True Christianity;* part of the time he stood up and admired the wonders of the sea; part of the time he talked to the sailors or wrote letters; and twice a day he preached from the stern to the red-coated soldiers.

Little by little he broke down the hostility of the officers until the captain graciously consented to let him use his own cabin when he wanted a little privacy. Never one to miss an opportunity to go ahead when the light was green, Whitefield laid a book entitled *The Self De-ceiver* on the captain's pillow, taking away the one that had been there. Next day the captain smilingly inquired who had made this exchange, and Whitefield pleaded guilty, urging him to read this helpful book.

Thenceforth the atmosphere on board ship visibly changed. "Blessed be God," wrote Whitefield, "we now live very comfortably in the great cabin. We talk of little else but God and Christ; and scarce a word is heard among us, when together, but what has reference to our fall in the first, and our new birth in the second Adam."

"Once, after a sermon," writes Whitefield's friend John Gillies, "Captain Mackay desired the soldiers to stop, whilst he informed them, that to his great shame, he had been a notorious swearer, but by the instrumen-tality of Mr. Whitefield's preaching he had now left it off—and exhorted them, for Christ's sake, to go and do likewise. The children were catechised, and there was a reformation throughout the whole soldiery. The women cried, 'What a change in our captain!' The bad books and packs of cards, which Mr. Whitefield exchanged for Bibles and other religious books, . . . were now thrown overboard."

Whitefield was only 23 years old at this time—a fact that makes this journey the more remarkable, for the youthful missionary had managed to collect and bring with him an immense store of supplies for the needy colonists of Georgia. The money and gifts were all received from friends in England who thus testified of their confidence in him.

Besides having what must have been a huge fund in those days, he brought with him clothing of all kinds for men, women, and children; a great variety of books, sewing materials, penknives, tinderboxes, tin pots, ink-horns, claw hammers, gun flints, gunpowder, scissors,

corkscrews, ivory combs, fishing tackle, drugs and med-
icines, stationery, sealing wax, quills and slate pencils;
besides many kinds of foodstuffs, including cheese, but-
ter, lemons and oranges (bought when the ship stopped
over at Gibraltar), spices, raisins, and sugar.

After his arrival in Savannah, Whitefield purchased
all sorts of additional supplies for the needy there. In the
long list of expenditures he carefully kept, we find such
items as a cow and a calf for a poor housekeeper, two
barrels of flour to set up a poor baker, and eight sows
with a boar for the poor of Highgate and Hampstead.

It was at this time that he conceived the idea of
establishing an orphanage in Georgia. On his return to
London he began collecting funds for it, and rented a
house for the orphans during his second visit to America.
Later, he managed to acquire five hundred acres and to
build a commodious and comfortable house for the children. He named the place Bethesda, and for thirty years
it was the object of his constant consideration. For its
support he was compelled to travel up and down the
land, in both England and America, preaching and solic-
iting funds.

Whitefield was continually accused by his opponents
of collecting the money for himself or of misusing the
funds. Often he was the butt of abuse and recrimination
in spite of the fact that he kept and made public a minute
account of the funds received and disbursed. "I hope to
be rich in heaven by taking care of orphans on earth. Any
other riches, blessed be God! are out of my view," he
said.

Bethesda was a house of refuge not only for homeless
orphans but also for widows and many destitute colonists. The frequent references that Whitefield made in
his correspondence to his "family" meant the occupants
of Bethesda, who sometimes numbered a hundred, only

about forty of whom were orphans.

A description of the orphanage, given by an enemy of Whitefield's, is rather interesting. He said: "Prepossessed with a bad opinion of the institution, I made all the enquiries I could, and, in short, became a convert to the design, which seems very conducive to the good of the infant colony. Whatever opinion I may have of the absurdity of some of their religious notions, tenets, and practices, yet, so far as they conduce to inculcate sobriety, industry, and frugality, they deserve encouragement from all well-wishers of the country. I could not here perceive anything of that spirit of uncharitableness and enthusiastic bigotry, for which their leader is so famed, and of which I heard shocking instances all over America."

Although the orphanage was so important in Whitefield's eyes, we realize that it was really a relatively insignificant part of the service he rendered. He was first, last, and always a preacher, and his unwearying labors in the evangelistic field are what loom largest. He made seven trips to America altogether—a lot of traveling when it is considered that each trip across the ocean took from one to four months.

Itinerating through the wilderness country of America was not without its hardships, and often Whitefield found it difficult to get enough to eat. Of a journey through Virginia he says: "Passed over two more ferries in the day's journey, and were put to some little inconvenience for want of finding a public-house in the way. However, at last we met a poor woman, who was going to sell cakes to the trained bands, of which we bought some; and, a few miles farther, a planter let us have some provender for our beasts, and a little milk . . . for ourselves. At six at night, we got to a place called Seals Church, twenty-nine miles from Potomac. Here we

called at a person's house to whom we were recommended; but the mistress of it was not at home, and the
overseer of the slaves, at first, was unwilling to receive
us. However, finding we were wet and strangers, he was
at last prevailed upon to let us abide there all night; and
furnished us with a good fire, with some little meat, and
milk, and a cake baked on the hearth, which was exceedingly refreshing, and afforded us no small matter for
praise and thanksgiving."

Sometimes on these journeys Whitefield would be
almost dead with heat and fatigue. Three times a day he
would have to be lifted up on his horse, for he had not
the strength to mount, but when he reached his destina-
tion he would preach in spite of his physical condition.
Sometimes he would preach in the fields, for many
churches were closed to him in America, as in England;
but always he had no difficulty getting an audience.

Whitefield was often sick, and one time he got out of
bed to preach, convinced that that sermon would be his
last. He spoke with unwonted energy, for he thought he
would be with his Master before the morning dawned.
After the sermon he was laid down on the ground by a
fire and he heard his friends say, "He is gone." But his
strength gradually returned to him, and as he lay there, a
black woman knelt by his side and said, "Master, you
just go to heaven's gate, but Jesus Christ said, 'Get you
down, you must not come here yet, but go first and call
some poor Negroes.'"

Whitefield's preaching made a profound impression
on many of the black slaves. He sometimes addressed
his remarks directly to them so that they were pricked to
the heart. "Have I a soul?" asked one of them.

Whitefield was not content merely to preach to them,
but made it a point to visit them in their homes. On such
visits he would pray for their sick and exhort old and

young. We get a pleasant little picture, from one of Whitefield's letters, of his kneeling down with the little black children and having them repeat the prayers after him. No wonder they loved him!

One time the members of a drinking club kept a black boy who for their diversion used to mimic people. The club members asked him to imitate Mr. Whitefield, but he refused to do so. When they insisted that he obey them, the boy stood before them and said, "I speak the truth in Christ, I lie not; unless you repent, you will all be damned." The impression made upon the members was so profound that the club never met again.

The appeal of Whitefield's message reached the bond and the free, the Southerners and the Northerners, the Puritans and the Presbyterians, the learned and the unlettered, white men and red men. To an Indian trader converted under his preaching and now desirous of becoming a missionary to the Indians, Whitefield gave this advice: "Frequently meditate on God's free love to yourself. That will best qualify you to speak of it affectionately to others."

The impression Whitefield made on Dr. Samuel Hopkins, then a young student at Yale, is interesting. He wrote: "The attention of the people in general was greatly awakened upon hearing the fame of him, that there was a remarkable preacher from England, traveling through the country. The people flocked to hear him when he came to New Haven. Some traveled twenty miles . . . to hear him. The assemblies were crowded, and remarkably attentive; people appeared generally to approve, and their conversation turned chiefly upon him and his preaching. . . . He preached against mixed dancing and the frolicking of males and females together; which practice was then very common in New England. This offended some, especially young people. But I remember I justified him in this in my own mind, and in conversation with those who were disposed to condemn him."

From Savannah to Boston, Whitefield itinerated, enduring hardships as a good soldier of the cross. "Seeing others do it who were as unable," he wrote, "I determined to inure myself to hardships, by lying constantly on the ground, which, by use, I found to be so far from being a hardship, that afterwards it became so to lie in a bed." His heart was always open to receive spiritual inspiration from any experience, even that of sleeping on the ground. One night as he looked into the flames of a fire kindled to keep off the wild beasts, he said, "It is an emblem of the divine love and presence keeping off evils and corruptions from the soul."

In Charleston, Whitefield met with his greatest success and his greatest opposition. The commissary, Alexander Garden, preached a vitriolic sermon against him. "His heart seemed full of choler and resentment," wrote Whitefield in his journal; "and, out of the abundance thereof, he poured forth so many bitter words against the Methodists . . . in general, and me in particular, that several, who intended to receive the Sacrament at his hands, withdrew. Never, I believe, was such a preparation sermon preached before. I could not help thinking the preacher was of the same spirit as Bishop Gardiner in Queen Mary's days."

Whitefield's fondness for the Dissenters, Baptists, Presbyterians, and any others whom he believed loved the Lord Jesus was a continual source of irritation to many of the bishops of the Established Church. Whitefield was noted for his lack of bigotry. He said, "When we confine the Spirit of God to this or that particular church, and are not willing to converse with any but those of the same communion, this is to be righteous overmuch with a witness; and so it is to confine our communion within church walls, and to think that Jesus could not be in a field, as well as on consecrated ground. This is Judaism; this is bigotry; this is like Peter, who would not go to preach the gospel to the Gentiles, till he had a vision sent from God.

"The Spirit of God is the centre of unity; and wherever I see the image of my Master, I never enquire of them their opinions: I ask them not what they are, so they love Jesus Christ in sincerity and truth; but embrace them as my brother, my sister, and my spouse. This is the spirit of Christianity.

"Many persons who are bigots to this or that opinion, when one of a different way of thinking has come where they were, have left the room or place on that account. This is the spirit of the devil; and, if it were possible that these persons could be admitted into heaven with these tempers, that very place would be a hell to them. Christianity will never flourish till we are all of one heart and one mind.

"This may be esteemed as enthusiasm and madness, and as a design to undermine the Established Church: no, God is my judge, I should rejoice to see all the world adhere to her articles. I am a friend to her articles. I am a friend to her homilies. I am a friend to her liturgy; and, if they did not thrust me out of their churches, I would read them every day; but I do not confine the Spirit of God there, for, I say it again, I love all that love the Lord Jesus Christ."

When some of the Covenanters in Scotland wanted him to preach only under their auspices, he said, "From giving way to the first risings of bigotry and a party spirit, good Lord, deliver us!"

In spite of the bigoted stand of Alexander Garden, Whitefield's preaching could not be stopped. Twice a day he preached to great crowds in Charleston, who met in the meetinghouses of the Baptists or Independents. The people were melted into tears, and could not bear to see Whitefield leave them for his trip to Beaufort, Port Royal, and Savannah.

In New England, Whitefield was generally received as an angel from God. His audiences consisted of as many as 23,000. But—to their shame be it said—the faculties of Yale and Harvard were his chief opponents. Said the Harvard professors, "We look upon Mr. Whitefield's going about in an itinerant way, especially as he has so much of an enthusiastical turn of mind, as being utterly inconsistent with the peace and order, if not the very being, of the churches of Christ." They referred to him as "an uncharitable, censorious, and slanderous man."

The faculty of Yale endorsed "the testimony of their brethren at Harvard." They were especially irked because, they said, Whitefield had stated that "the generality of ministers were unconverted, and that all unconverted ministers were half beasts and half devils, and could no more be the means of any man's conversion than a dead man could beget living children."

There was quite a paper warfare as many ministers and friends came to Whitefield's defense. The aftermath came twenty-nine years later when Whitefield, learning that the Harvard library had been destroyed by fire, begged books and was enabled to procure large benefactions for it. This was at a time when Dr. Wigglesworth, who had been one of his leading opponents, was still professor there. On the official records of the college Whitefield's kindness is noted, and this statement appears: "It was voted that the thanks of this corporation be given to the Reverend Mr. Whitefield, for these instances of candour and generosity."

Thus, on all his trips to America, Whitefield's labors were very fruitful. In his characteristic way, he wrote to Wesley, "If you ask, how it is with me? I answer, 'Happy in Jesus, the Lord my righteousness.' If you ask, what I am doing? I answer, 'Ranging and hunting in the American woods after poor sinners.' If you ask, with what success? I would answer, 'My labours were never more acceptable; and the door, for fifteen hundred miles together, is quite open for preaching the everlasting gospel.' Congregations are large, and the work is going on, just as it began and went on in England."

He was an American at heart, and found much happiness in his work here. To his mother he wrote, "I love to range in the American woods, and sometimes think I shall never return to England."

Friendship With Benjamin Franklin

Among the famous contemporaries and admirers of George Whitefield we find Benjamin Franklin, whose life spanned most of the eighteenth century. Franklin was in his thirties when Whitefield, in his early twenties, first preached in Philadelphia. In his *Autobiography* the author of *Poor Richard's Almanack* gives his impression of Whitefield's preaching: "The multitudes of all sects and denominations that attended his sermons were enormous, and it was a matter of speculation to me, who was one of the number, to observe the extraordinary influence of his oratory on his hearers, and how much they admired and respected him, notwithstanding his common abuse of them, by assuring them they were naturally *half beasts and half devils*. It was wonderful to see the change soon made in the manners of our inhabitants. From being thoughtless and indifferent about religion, it seemed as if all the world were growing religious, so that one could not walk through . . . [Philadelphia] in an evening without hearing psalms sung in different families of every street."

In his newspaper, Franklin ended an account of Whitefield's preaching by stating, "On Sunday, at Whiteclay Creek, he preached twice, resting about half an hour between the sermons, to about eight thousand, of whom three thousand, it is computed, came on horseback. It rained most of the time, and yet they stood in the open air.''

A warm friendship sprang up between these two men, although it did not result in Franklin's becoming a born-again Christian, as Whitefield so much desired and prayed.

In the following year when Whitefield was again preaching in Philadelphia, Franklin was so carried away with his eloquence that he gave liberally to the Orphan House after having determined to contribute nothing at all. In his *Autobiography,* Franklin tells the story: "Returning northward, he [Mr. Whitefield] preached up this charity and made large collections; for his eloquence had a wonderful power over the hearts and purses of his hearers, of which I myself was an instance. I did not disapprove of the design; but as Georgia was then destitute of materials and workmen and it was proposed to send them from Philadelphia at a great expense, I thought it would have been better to have built the house at Philadelphia and brought the children to it. This I advised; but he was resolute in his first project, rejected my counsel, and I therefore refused to contribute.

"I happened soon after to attend one of his sermons, in the course of which I perceived he intended to finish with a collection, and I silently resolved that he should get nothing from me. I had in my pocket a handful of copper money, three or four silver dollars, and five pistoles in gold. As he proceeded I began to soften and concluded to give the copper. Another stroke of his oratory . . . determined me to give the silver; and he finished so admirably that I emptied my pocket wholly into the collector's dish, gold and all.

"At this sermon there was also one of our club who, being of my sentiments respecting the building in Georgia and suspecting a collection might be intended, had by precaution emptied his pockets before he came from home. Toward the conclusion of the discourse, however, he felt a strong inclination to give, and applied to a neighbor who stood near him to lend him money for the purpose. The request was fortunately made to perhaps the only man in the company who had the firmness not to be affected by the preacher. His answer was, 'At any other time, friend Hopkinson, I would lend to thee freely, but not now, for thee seems to be out of thy right senses.' "

Franklin defended Whitefield from the charge of his enemies that the money collected for the orphans went into his own pocket. Franklin writes: "Some of Mr. Whitefield's enemies affected to suppose that he would apply these collections to his own private emolument; but I, who was intimately acquainted with him, being employed in printing his sermons and journals, never had the least suspicion of his integrity, but am to this day decidedly of opinion that he was in all his conduct a perfectly *honest man;* and methinks my testimony in his favor ought to have the more weight, as we had no religious connection. He used, indeed, sometimes to pray for my conversion, but he never had the satisfaction of believing that his prayers were heard. Ours was a mere civil friendship, sincere on both sides, and lasted to his death."

"The following instance," adds Franklin, "will show the terms on which we stood. Upon one of his arrivals from England at Boston he wrote to me that he should come soon to Philadelphia, but knew not where he could lodge when there, as he understood his old friend and host, Mr. Benezet, was removed to Germantown. My answer was: 'You know my house; if you can make shift with its scanty accommodations, you will be most heartily welcome.' He replied that if I made that kind offer for

Christ's sake I should not miss of a reward. And I returned: 'Don't let me be mistaken; it was not for *Christ's* sake, but for *your* sake.'"

Franklin was curious to know just how far Whitefield's voice carried as he preached outdoors, and in Franklin's characteristically thorough way, he went about making calculations. He tells about it in his *Autobiography:* "He had a loud and clear voice, and articulated his words so perfectly that he might be heard and understood at a great distance, especially as his auditors observed the most perfect silence. He preached one evening from the top of the court-house steps, which are in the middle of Market Street and on the west side of Second Street, which crosses it at right angles. Both streets were filled with his hearers to a considerable distance. Being among the hindmost in Market Street, I had the curiosity to learn how far he could be heard by retiring backward down the street toward the river; and I found his voice distinct till I came near Front Street, when some noise in that street obscured it. Imagining then a semicircle, of which my distance should be the radius, and that it was filled with auditors to each of whom I allowed two square feet, I computed that he might well be heard by more than thirty thousand. This reconciled me to the newspaper accounts of his having preached to twenty-five thousand people in the fields, and to the history of generals haranguing whole armies, of which I had sometimes doubted."

As a footnote to his memoirs, Franklin tells an anecdote concerning a drummer who intended to drown out Whitefield's voice: "In the early part of his life Mr. Whitefield was preaching in an open field, when a drummer happened to be present who was determined to interrupt his pious business, and rudely beat his drum in a violent manner in order to drown the preacher's voice.

Mr. Whitefield spoke very loud, but was not as powerful as the instrument. He therefore called out to the drummer in these words: 'Friend, you and I serve the two greatest masters existing, but in different callings; you beat up for volunteers for King George, I for the Lord Jesus. In God's name, then, let us not interrupt each other; the world is wide enough for both, and we may get recruits in abundance.' This speech had such an effect on the drummer that he went away in great good humor, and left the preacher in full possession of the field."

Whitefield retained hopes that Franklin would accept Christ as his personal Saviour. In 1740 the 25-year-old preacher wrote:

"Dear Mr. Franklin,

"I thank you for your letter. You may print my life, as you desire. God willing, I shall correct my two volumes of sermons, and send them the very first opportunity. Pray write to me by every ship that goes shortly to Charleston. . . .

"Dear sir, adieu! I do not despair of your seeing the reasonableness of Christianity. Apply to God; be willing to do the Divine will, and you shall know it. Oh! the love of God to your unworthy friend,

"George Whitefield"

Some years later Franklin ventured to give his friend some advice in regard to the advantages of winning the rich to his cause:

"I am glad to hear that you have frequent opportunities of preaching among the great. If you can gain them to a good and exemplary life, wonderful change will follow in the manners of the lower ranks; for *ad exemplum regis,* et cetera. On this principle, Confucius, the famous eastern reformer, proceeded. When he saw his country sunk in vice, and wickedness of all kinds triumphant, he applied himself first to the grandees; and, having, by his doctrine, won them to the cause of virtue, the commons followed in multitudes.

"The mode has a wonderful influence on mankind; and there are numbers, who, perhaps, fear less the being in hell, than out of the fashion. Our more western reformations began with the ignorant mob; and, when numbers of them were gained, interest and party-views drew in the wise and great. Where both methods can be used, reformations are likely to be more speedy. O that some method could be found to make them lasting! He who discovers that, will, in my opinion, deserve more, ten thousand times, than the inventor of the longitude.

"My wife and family join in the most cordial salutations to you and good Mrs. Whitefield.

"I am, dear sir, your very affectionate friend, and most obliged humble servant,

"Benjamin Franklin"

At this time there was a good deal of correspondence between these two distinguished men when Franklin arranged for the purchase of Whitefield's meetinghouse in Philadelphia in connection with the establishment of the College of Philadelphia. This college has since grown into the University of Pennsylvania.

Whitefield feared that the most important element of education would be too casually treated in the institution, and therefore wrote to Franklin:

"My dear Mr. Franklin,

"I am glad that the gentlemen of Philadelphia are exerting their efforts to erect an academy. I have often thought such an institution was exceedingly wanted; and I am persuaded, if well conducted, it will be of public service. I have read your plan, and do not wonder at its meeting with general approbation. . . .

"It is true you say, 'The youth are to be taught some public religion, and the excellency of the Christian religion in particular'; but me thinks this is mentioned too late, and too soon passed over. As we are all creatures of a day, as our whole life is but one small point between two eternities, it is reasonable to suppose that the grand end of every Christian institution for forming tender minds should be to convince them of their natural depravity, of the means of recovering out of it, and of the necessity of preparing for the enjoyment of the Supreme Being in a future state. These are the grand points in which Christianity centres. Arts and science may be built on this, and serve to embellish the superstructure, but without this there cannot be any good foundation.''

In this letter Whitefield put his finger on the great point of departure between the two men concerning education. Franklin would present "some public religion" as an embellishment of the arts and sciences; Whitefield would make Christ the beginning, the middle, and the end of all teaching, knowing full well that great and glorious enlightenment in other fields would almost automatically follow.

As the years passed, Franklin became increasingly renowned, but the friendship between the two men continued unabated. Faithfully and without fawning, Whitefield pleaded with his friend to study a mystery of far greater portent than electricity. In 1752 he wrote: "Dear Mr. Franklin,

"I find that you grow more and more famous in the learned world. As you have made a pretty considerable progress in the mysteries of electricity, I would now humbly recommend to your diligent unprejudiced pursuit and study the mystery of the new birth. It is a most important, interesting study, and, when mastered, will richly repay you for all your pains. One, at whose bar we are shortly to appear, hath solemnly declared, that, without it we cannot 'enter into the kingdom of heaven.'

You will excuse this freedom. I must have *aliquid Christi** in all my letters.

"I am yet a willing pilgrim for His great name's sake, and I trust a blessing attends my poor feeble labours. To the Giver of every good gift be all the glory! My respects await yourself and all enquiring friends; and hoping to see you once more in the land of the living, I subscribe myself, dear sir, your very affectionate friend, and obliged servant,

"George Whitefield"

We have no record of a reply to this plea, but a few years later, in 1756, Franklin wrote concerning a scheme he wished might be tried out—the settling of a colony in Ohio by himself and Whitefield. His letter follows:
"Dear Sir,

"I received your favour of the twenty-fourth of February with great pleasure, as it informed me of your welfare, and expressed your continued regard for me. I thank you for the pamphlet you enclosed to me. As we had just observed a provincial fast on the same occasion, I thought it very seasonable to be published in Pennsylvania; and accordingly reprinted it immediately.

"You mention your frequent wish that you were a chaplain to the American army. I sometimes wish that you and I were jointly employed by the Crown to settle a colony on the Ohio. I imagine that we could do it effectually, and without putting the nation to much expense; but, I fear, we shall never be called upon for such a service.

"What a glorious thing it would be to settle in that fine country a large, strong body of religious and industrious people! What a security to the other colonies, and advantage to Britain, by increasing her people, territory,

* "something of Christ"

strength, and commerce! Might it not greatly facilitate the introduction of pure religion among the heathen, if we could, by such a colony, shew them a better sample of Christians than they commonly see in our Indian traders? [They are] the most vicious and abandoned wretches of our nation!

"Life, like a dramatic piece, should not only be conducted with regularity, but, methinks, it should finish handsomely. . . . In such an enterprise, I could spend the remainder of life with pleasure: and I firmly believe God would bless us with success, if we undertook it with a sincere regard to His honour, the service of our gracious king, and (which is the same thing) the public good. . . .

"I thank you for your good wishes and prayers; and am, with the greatest esteem and affection, dear sir, your most obedient humble servant,

"Benjamin Franklin
"My best respects to Mrs. Whitefield."

Of course, that colony was never established by Whitefield and Franklin, for now there were heard in England and America the rumblings of the great War of Independence. In 1768, as Franklin contemplated the ominous international situation he wrote skeptically to Whitefield:

"I *see* with you that our affairs are not well managed by our rulers here below; I wish I could *believe* with you, that they are well attended to by those above; I rather suspect, from certain circumstances, that though the general government of the universe is well administered, our particular little affairs are perhaps below notice, and left to take the chance of human prudence or imprudence, as either may happen to be uppermost. It is, however, an uncomfortable thought, and I leave it."

Whitefield's reaction to this was, *Uncomfortable*, indeed! and, blessed be God, *unscriptural;* for we are fully assured that 'the Lord reigneth,' and are directed to cast *all* our care on Him, because He careth for us."

It is sad to note that Benjamin Franklin, with all his intelligence, never had the wisdom to discern or the simplicity of heart to believe the gospel message of salvation through faith. A letter he wrote to the president of Yale during the last year of his life, when he was 84 years old, indicates that he felt his good works would carry him through, and that he built his hopes on that most flimsy foundation. The letter also shows that he questioned the divinity of Christ. Here is his statement:

"You desire to know something of my religion. It is the first time I have been questioned upon it. But I cannot take your curiosity amiss, and shall endeavor in a few words to gratify it. Here is my creed. I believe in one God, the creator of the universe. That He governs it by His providence. That He ought to be worshiped. That the most acceptable service we render to Him is doing good to His other children. That the soul of man is immortal and will be treated with justice in another life respecting its conduct in this. These I take to be the fundamental points in all sound religion, and I regard them as you do in whatever sect I meet with them.

"As to Jesus of Nazareth, my opinion of whom you particularly desire, I think His system of morals and His religion, as He lent them to us, the best the world ever saw or is like to see; but I apprehend it has received various corrupting changes, and I have, with most of the present Dissenters in England, some doubts as to His divinity; though it is a question I do not dogmatize upon, having never studied it, and think it needless to busy myself with it now, when I expect soon an opportunity of knowing the truth with less trouble. . . .

"I shall only add, respecting myself, that, having experienced the goodness of that Being in conducting me prosperously through a long life, I have no doubt of its continuance in the next, though without the smallest conceit of meriting such goodness.''

The tribute Franklin paid to Whitefield after hearing of his death is not without interest. Writing to a friend, Franklin said, ''I cannot forbear expressing the pleasure it gives me to see an account of the respect paid to Mr. Whitefield's memory by your assembly. I knew him intimately upwards of thirty years. His integrity, disinterestedness, and indefatigable zeal in prosecuting every good work, I have never seen equalled, and shall never see excelled.''

Impact on Other Famous Contemporaries

He seems to be a very good man, and one who truly desires the salvation of mankind. God grant that the wisdom of the serpent may be joined to the innocence of the dove!" wrote the incomparable Susannah Wesley to her son Samuel after her meeting with Whitefield.

It is interesting to note the impression that Whitefield made on some of his famous contemporaries. The reaction of Samuel Johnson to the man who had been his fellow student at Pembroke College was somewhat frivolous. According to Boswell, the great lexicographer said, "Whitefield's popularity is chiefly owing to the peculiarity of his manner. He would be followed by crowds, were he to wear a nightcap in the pulpit, or were he to preach from a tree." Strongly loyal to the Church of England, Johnson was no doubt shocked at the temerity of a minister who would preach in the open fields. But he said, "I never treated Whitefield's ministry with contempt: I belive he did good. He devoted himself to the lower classes of mankind, and among them he was of use."

The wife of Jonathan Edwards (whose sermon "Sinners in the Hands of an Angry God" is said to have pulled many out of the fire) wrote enthusiastically: "Dear Brother James:

"I want to prepare you for a visit from the Reverend

Mr. Whitefield, the famous preacher of England. He has been sojourning with us and, after visiting a few of the neighbouring towns, is going to New Haven, and from thence to New York. He is truly a remarkable man, and, during his visit, has, I think, verified all that we have heard of him. He makes less of the doctrines than our American preachers generally do, and aims more at affecting the heart. He is a born orator. You have already heard of his deep-toned, yet clear and melodious, voice. It is perfect music.

"It is wonderful to see what a spell he casts over an audience by proclaiming the simplest truths of the Bible. I have seen upwards of a thousand people hang on his words with breathless silence, broken only by an occasional half-suppressed sob. He impresses the ignorant, and not less the educated and refined. It is reported that while the miners of England listened to him, the tears made white furrows down their smutty cheeks. So here, our mechanics shut up their shops, and the day-labourers throw down their tools, to go and hear him preach, and few return unaffected.

"A prejudiced person, I know, might say that this is all theatrical artifice and display; but not so will any one think who has seen and known him. He is a very devout and godly man, and his only aim seems to be to reach and influence men the best way. He speaks from a heart all aglow with love, and pours out a torrent of eloquence which is almost irresistible. I wish him success in his apostlic career; and, when he reaches New Haven, you will, I know, shew him warm hospitality.

"Yours, in faithful affection,
"Sarah"

Sarah's husband, the great Calvinist himself, wrote as follows:

"Mr. Whitefield came to Northampton about the

middle of October, 1740, and preached four sermons in the meetinghouse. The congregation was extraordinarily melted by every sermon; almost the whole assembly being in tears. His sermons were suitable to the circumstances of the town; containing just reproofs of our backslidings; and, in a most moving and affecting manner, making use of our great mercies as arguments with us to return to God, from whom we had departed.

"Immediately after this, the minds of the people in general appeared more engaged in religion. The revival at first was principally among professors, to whom Mr. Whitefield had chiefly addressed himself; but, in a short time, there was a deep concern among young persons."

This was the impression that Whitefield made on people who loved the Word of God. What sort of an impression would he make on an infidel? He was a contemporary of David Hume, the author of *An Enquiry Concerning Human Understanding.* It is not to be doubted that the preaching of Whitefield and the Wesleys was largely accountable for the cold reception Hume's work received when he returned from Italy expecting the plaudits of the public. Nevertheless, Hume did not consider twenty miles too far to travel to hear Whitefield.

"Once," said he, "Whitefield addressed his audience thus: 'The attendant angel is about to leave us, and ascend to heaven. Shall he ascend and not bear with him the news of one sinner reclaimed from the error of his way?' And, then, stamping with his foot, and lifting up his hands and eyes to heaven, he cried aloud, 'Stop, Gabriel, stop, ere you enter the sacred portals, and yet carry with you the tidings of one sinner being saved.' This address surpassed anything I ever saw or heard in any other preacher."

The famous actor David Garrick, who was also the manager of the celebrated Drury Lane Theatre, was another who was tremendously moved, though not converted, by the eloquence of Whitefield. The actor claimed that the preacher could make men weep or tremble according to the way he pronounced *Mesopotamia.* "I would give a hundred guineas," said Garrick, "if I could only say 'Oh!' like Mr. Whitefield."

Whitefield remarked that "few have either courage or conduct to head a Christian party amongst persons of high life," but there were a surprising number of aristocrats and even members of the royal family who attended his sermons, and not a few of them were converted. Wesley preached the gospel almost exclusively to the poor, and the poor heard him gladly; but it was Whitefield's task to reach the rich, as well, and a number heard and believed.

Among his hearers were the Duchess of Marlborough; the Duchess of Buckingham; the Duke of Bolton; Lord Hervey, keeper of the privy seal; the Duke of Cumberland, youngest son of George II; and even Frederick, Prince of Wales. A host of titled women, too numerous to mention here, were of that company who emulated the "honourable women. . . , not a few" who believed in Paul's time.

Of some of his contacts with "Caesar's household," Whitefield wrote to a friend: "My hands have been full of work, and I have been among great company. A privy counsellor of the King of Denmark, and others, with one of the Prince of Wales's favourites, dined and drank tea with me on Monday. On Tuesday, I preached twice at Lady Huntingdon's, to several of the nobility. In the morning, the Earl of Chesterfield was present. In the evening, Lord Bolingbroke. All behaved quite well, and were in some degree affected.

"Lord Chesterfield thanked me, and said, 'Sir, I will not tell you what I shall tell others, how I approve of you,' or words to this purpose. He conversed with me freely afterwards. Lord Bolingbroke was much moved, and desired I would come and see him next morning. I did; and his lordship behaved with great candour and frankness. All accepted of my sermons.''

Lord Chesterfield, of whom Dr. Johnson once remarked that he was a wit among lords and a lord among wits, later wrote to Lady Huntingdon his impressions of Whitefield: ''Mr. Whitefield's eloquence is unrivalled—his zeal inexhaustible; and not to admire both would argue a total absence of taste, and an insensibility not to be coveted by anybody. Your ladyship is a powerful auxiliary to the Methodist Cabinet; and I confess, notwithstanding my own private feelings and sentiments, I am infinitely pleased at your zeal in so good a cause.''

Whitefield recounts an amusing comment that King George II made to his half-sister, Lady Chesterfield. ''His Majesty seems to have been acquainted with some things about us, by what passed in his discourse with Lady Chesterfield. The particulars are these. Her ladyship wore a suit of clothes, with a brown ground and silver flowers. His Majesty, coming round to her, first smiled, and then laughed quite out. Her ladyship could not imagine what was the cause of this. At length, His Majesty said, 'I know who chose that gown for you— Mr. Whitefield. I hear that you have attended on him this year and a half.' Her ladyship answered, 'Yes, I have, and like him very well.' ''

Lord Bolingbroke also liked him very well, and wrote his opinion to the Countess of Huntingdon:

''Mr. Whitefield is the most extraordinary man in our times. He has the most commanding eloquence I ever heard in any person; his abilities are very considerable; his zeal unquenchable; and his piety and excellence genuine—unquestionable.

"The bishops and inferior orders of the clergy are very angry with him, and endeavour to represent him as a hypocrite, an enthusiast; but this is not astonishing—there is so little real goodness or honesty among them. Your Ladyship will be somewhat amused at hearing that the king has represented to His Grace of Canterbury, that Mr. Whitefield should be advanced to the Bench, as the only means of putting an end to his preaching. What a keen, what a biting remark! but how just, and how well earned by those mitred lords!''

Thus the gospel was preached as a witness to all classes so that none might be without excuse in the day of judgment. Scientists, statesmen, aristocrats, writers, and men and women from all walks of life had the opportunity of hearing the glad tidings, and many believed.

Marriage

The Lord has given me a wife. Her name was James, a widow, between 30 and 40 years of age. She has been a housekeeper many years. Once gay; but, for three years last past, a despised follower of the Lamb of God. I left her about three weeks ago, and am going to settle affairs, and bring her up to London.''

Elizabeth James might not have been too pleased if she had known her husband stated her age as "between 30 and 40." She was actually 36, and that was old enough when one considers that her youthful husband was ten years younger. But she was evidently a well-balanced woman of good judgment, and there is every reason to believe that the marriage was as happy as it could be with the itinerating husband away months at a time.

Elizabeth was a good friend of John Wesley's, having entertained him in her home in Abergavenny (Wales) on various occasions. "In the afternoon we came to Abergavenny," Wesley writes in his journal. "Those who are bitter of spirit have been here also; yet Mrs. James (now Mrs. Whitefield) received us gladly, as she had done aforetime." He spoke of her, not without reason, as "a woman of candour and humanity."

Whitefield describes her as "neither rich in fortune, nor beautiful as to her person, but, I believe, a true child of God, and one who would not, I think, attempt to hinder me in His work for the world. . . . I hope God will never suffer me to say, 'I have married a wife, and therefore I cannot come.' ''

Wesley and Whitefield both took the stand that any woman who married either of them would have to be content to be left alone a good deal while they journeyed from place to place, publishing the good tidings of peace. It is questionable whether either of them should have married under the circumstances. Surely to such especially endowed men, Paul's admonition could be applied: ''I say therefore to the unmarried and widows, It is good for them if they abide even as I.'' The hearts of these men were bound up in their work with a fervor that could only be produced and maintained by the unction of the Spirit. To them marriage must necessarily have been little more than a distraction, and at times even a hindrance.

Whitefield hinted at this in a letter he wrote to a young man seeking advice about getting married: ''If you marry, let it be in the Lord, and for the Lord, and then the Lord will give it His blessing. Only remember this, marry when or whom you will, expect trouble in the flesh. But I spare you.''

Although Whitefield's wife was not, like Wesley's, a jealous and discontented troublemaker, she evidently found it difficult at times to be reconciled to her lonely life. One time Whitefield was traveling from Charleston to Bermuda and had left Elizabeth behind, intending to return to her several months later, in the fall. But as he was boarding a ship, a letter from England made him feel that it was imperative for him to go there via New England after finishing his tour in the Bermudas. This, of course, would preclude his seeing his wife in Charleston. He wrote to his friend, ''I have a great mind to come to you from New England. But what will . . . [my wife] say?

I have left her behind me in the tent; and, should I bring her to England, my two families, in America, must be left without a head. Should I go without her, I fear, the trial will be too hard for her; but, if the Lord calls, I can put both her and myself into His all-bountiful hands.''
"My dear wife will have a trial in my being absent.''

Whitefield longed, as Luther had longed, to have a son who would follow in his steps as an evangelist, but, like Luther, he was to be disappointed. A couple of years after his marriage, his wife presented him with a son, but thrilled as he was at the birth of the little one, he nevertheless stayed home only long enough to baptize him. Then, for the next seven weeks, he continued his journeyings as indefatigably as ever.

Four months later the baby died, and the grief-stricken father wrote to a friend:

"Who knows what a day may bring forth? Last night, I was called to sacrifice my Isaac; I mean, to bury my only child and son, about four months old.

"Many things had occurred to make me believe he was, not only to be continued to me, but, to be a preacher of the everlasting gospel. Pleased with the thought, and being ambitious of having a son of my own so divinely employed, Satan was permitted to give me some wrong impressions, whereby, as I now find, I misapplied several texts of Scripture. Upon these grounds, I made no scruple of declaring 'that I should have a son, and that his name was to be John.' I mentioned the very time of his birth, and fondly hoped that he was to be great in the sight of the Lord.

"Everything happened according to the predictions, and my wife having had several narrow escapes while pregnant, especially by her falling from a high horse, and my driving her into a deep ditch in a one-horse chaise a little before the time of her lying-in, and from which we received little or no hurt, confirmed me in my expectation, that God would grant me my heart's desire.

"Housekeeping being expensive in London, I thought it best to send both parent and child to Abergavenny, where my wife had a little house, the furniture of which, as I thought of soon embarking for Georgia, I had partly sold, and partly given away. In their journey thither, they stopped at Gloucester, at the Bell Inn, which my brother now keeps, and in which I was born. There, my beloved was cut off with a stroke. Upon my coming here, without knowing what had happened, I enquired concerning the welfare of parent and child; and, by the answer, found that the flower was cut down.

"I immediately called all to join in prayer, in which I blessed the Father of mercies for giving me a son, continuing it to me so long, and taking it from me so soon. All joined in desiring that I would decline preaching till the child was buried; but I remembered a saying of good Mr. Henry, 'that weeping must not hinder sowing'; and, therefore, I preached twice the next day, and also the day following; on the evening of which, just as I was closing my sermon, the bell struck out for the funeral.

"At first, I must acknowledge, it gave nature a little shake; but, looking up, I recovered strength, and then concluded with saying, that this text, on which I had been preaching, namely, 'All things work together for good to them that love God,' made me as willing to go out to my son's funeral, as to hear of his birth."

Doubtless because of the age of his wife, her poor health, and the tremendous infant mortality rate of those times, Whitefield never had a child that lived long after birth.

Somtimes Elizabeth was able to accompany her husband in his travels, and it was evidently a joyful experience for both of them. On one such occasion he wrote to a friend, "My wife and I go on like two happy pilgrims, leaning upon our Beloved."

A letter that Elizabeth wrote to the Countess of Huntingdon gives us a glimpse into her deep spiritual experience:
"Honoured Madam,

"I am almost ashamed to write to your ladyship now; but have not been able to write sooner. I have been so ill since I came home, that Dr. Lobb and Dr. Nisbett have attended me, more or less, ever since. I was in bed when I received your ladyship's letter, and was not able to read it. I had a pleuritic fever, and was so low that the doctor durst not bleed me. I am glad to hear, by Mr. Smith, that your ladyship is so well. God be praised! O may the good Lord give your ladyship a prosperous soul in a healthy body, to His own glory, and the good of very many poor souls!

"Your ladyship was heard of God's goodness to my dear honoured master in Ireland. A gentleman writes me thus: 'Dear Mr. Whitefield has left Dublin very sorrowful. His going away is lamented by many of all denominations,' et cetera, since the twenty-second of June.

"Here are letters from Georgia, bringing good and bad news; the good, they are all well; the bad, they run him behind very much. But all is well. The Lord has been and is exceedingly good to us at the poor Tabernacle, and lets it often be filled with His glory.

"O dear madam, what am I, and what my father's house, that I am so highly favoured to be called a child of God! Oh, to be a *child!* Dear, dear madam, I am almost lost in thought. What! to have the great Jehovah, the God of heaven and earth, to be my Father; to make my bed in my sickness; to be afflicted in all my affliction; to support me in and under all my trials and temptations, and to make His abode with me! Thinking of this has sometimes been too much for my weak nature to bear. Oh, for the time when we shall be dissolved, and be forever with the Lord!''

There are many references to his wife in Whitefield's letters. Returning home, he would write to a friend, "I found my poor wife an invalid. Our Lord can restore her, for He came to heal our sicknesses, and to bear our infirmities.'' Again, from Lisbon he wrote, "O pray for me; and add to my obligations by frequently visiting my poor wife. Kindnesses shewn to her, during my absence, will be double kindnesses.''

On another occasion he wrote from Bermuda, "They have loaded me with provisions for my sea store; and in the several parishes, by a private voluntary contribution, have raised me upwards of one hundred pounds sterling. This will pay a little of Bethesda's debt, and enable me to make such a remittance to my dear yokefellow, as may keep her from being embarrassed, or too much beholden in my absence.''

A month before the death of Elizabeth, Whitefield was in Edinburgh. He wrote at that time to a friend, "As you do not mention my wife, I suppose she is out of town.'' He returned to London shortly after, only to find his wife sick with the fever from which she never recovered. Whitefield himself preached her funeral sermon, and in it paid tribute to her fortitude, showing how she had once bolstered his failing courage. Said he: "Do you remember my preaching in those fields by the old stump of a tree? The multitude was great, and many were disposed to be riotous. At first, I addressed them firmly; but when a desperate gang drew near, with the more ferocious and horrid imprecations and menaces, my courage began to fail. My wife was then standing behind me, as I stood on the table. I think I hear her now. She pulled my gown, and looking up, said, 'George, play the man for your God.' My confidence returned. I spoke to the multitude with boldness and affection. They became still, and many were deeply affected.''

In Tottenham Court Road a monument was erected bearing an inscription that sounds as if it had been written by Whitefield himself: "To the memory of Mrs. Whitefield, who, after thirty years' strong and frequent manifestations of her Redeemer's love, mixed with strong and frequent strugglings against the buffetings of Satan, and many sicknesses and indwellings of sin, was joyfully released, August 9, 1769.''

Mrs. Whitefield's death occurred when she was 64 years old and had been married to Whitefield twenty-eight years.

Lady Huntingdon

Lady Selina Huntingdon was visiting the humble room of the distressed wife of a soldier, carrying to her some much needed food and clothing. As the visitor ministered to the woman materially, she called her attention to the living Bread that came down from heaven, and urged her to partake of that, also. The room in which she was visiting was next to a bakery where the employees heard the conversation through a crack in the wall. They begged Lady Huntingdon to teach them also, and soon a little company of women gathered every day to hear her expound the Scriptures.

A blacksmith notorious for his wickedness thought he would enjoy creating a disturbance among the women and so followed them into the room where they met, and sat in a corner, waiting for an opportunity to disconcert the speaker. When Lady Huntingdon saw him, she thought she would ask him to leave, but changed her mind and decided to ignore him. The man listened with more attention than he planned to give to the searching study of the countess, and forgetting his original purpose, sought only to find the answer to the question "What shall I do that I may inherit eternal life?" Since the promise is that those who ask receive, the blasphemer found what he lacked, was converted, and lived many years longer to honor the Master he once scorned.

Lady Huntingdon—a distant relative of George Washington's—was one of the noble women raised up to give assistance and encouragement to Whitefield and others in their work of revival. Though it is true that "not many mighty, not many noble, are called," and that "it is easier for a camel to go through the eye of a needle, than for a rich man to enter into the kingdom of God," yet it was the happy experience of Whitefield to attract to the gospel a number of illustrious men and women who gave his work both moral and financial support. Among these, Lady Huntingdon was outstanding.

A true mother in Israel, the countess believed in a faith that works, and was not given to a rocking-chair type of religion. "The folding of the hands, a sweet retirement into unworldly places, a graceful withdrawal from forbidden things, was not *her* testimony to the exceeding sinfulness of sin. She went from the altar and the mercy seat warmed with holy zeal; her presence aroused the moral consciousness of the most dormant; her whole life was a constant exhortation, 'Turn ye, turn ye . . . ; for why will ye die?' " The warmth of her ardor was the more remarkable inasmuch as zeal even in the pulpit was an unpardonable sin in her day when "dead" men were preaching dead sermons to people dead in sins.

Many were the souls converted through her efforts. She particularly looked upon the employees on her estate as special charges whom she must win to the Master, and she spent a part of every day with them. One day she said to one of her workers, "Thomas, I fear you never pray, or look to Christ for salvation."

"Your ladyship is mistaken," he replied. "I heard what passed between you and James at the garden wall, and the word you meant for him took effect on me."

"How did you hear it?" she asked.

"I heard it on the other side of the garden, through a

hole in the wall, and I shall never forget the impression I received."

It is not surprising that Lady Huntingdon was such a successful soul winner, for the secret was revealed in a letter she wrote to Charles Wesley in which she said, "I am rarely if ever out of the presence of God. He is a pillar of light before me."

One time as she walked down the street, a woman approached her and said, "Oh, madam, you are come."

Astonished at such a greeting from a total stranger, the countess asked, "What do you know of me?"

"Madam, I saw you in a dream three years ago, dressed as you now are," the woman replied, and related other aspects of the dream. Lady Huntingdon was quick to take advantage of the unusual experience by leading her new friend to Christ, and a year later the woman died happy in her new-found faith.

It was through the Countess of Huntingdon that Whitefield was enabled to reach so many of the nobility of England. When he was 30 years of age she invited him to preach at her home in Chelsea, and there he was able to speak to many fashionable and aristocratic congregations. And while he spoke to the lords and ladies in the drawing room of the countess, the servants in the kitchen also listened attentively.

Describing one of these meetings, Lady Huntingdon wrote to a friend: "It was a time of refreshing from the presence of our God. Several of our little circle have been wonderfully filled with the love of God, and have had joy unspeakable and full of glory. Lady Frances is rejoicing in hope of the glory of God. It is impossible to conceive of more real happiness than she enjoys. Dear Mr. Whitefield's sermons and exhortations were close, searching, experimental, awful, and awakening. Surely God was with him. He appeared to speak of spiritual and divine things as awful realities. Many of us could witness to the truth of what he uttered. His discourses in the neighbouring churches were attended with power from on high, and the kingdom of darkness trembled before the gospel of Christ.''

One of the most remarkable features of Lady Huntingdon's character was her lack of covetousness. The love of money, "the root of all evil," found no place in her heart. She was the antithesis of the rich young ruler who went away sorrowful, loath to part with his possessions.

Noting that a godly group of people were meeting in Brighton in an "upper room" and wishing to strengthen their hands, she determined to build a chapel for them. Her gifts to charity had been so generous that she wondered where she would get the necessary means for this project. But as she glanced at her collection of jewelry, it occurred to her that it would be better to have treasure in heaven than in her jewel box, so she sold her precious ornaments for 698 pounds and erected a neat house of worship for the believers.* At great personal sacrifice, she established many chapels in England and saw to it that they were manned with Spirit-filled preachers.

One of her chaplains wrote of her sacrifices: "How do works, the works of faith and love, speak and preach Jesus Christ, in that devoted servant of His. No equipage, no livery servants, no house, all these given up, that perishing sinners may hear the life-giving sound, and be enriched with all spiritual blessings. Her prayers are heard, her chapel is crowded, and many sinners among the poor are brought to the city of refuge.''

---

* It will help the reader to get an idea of the relative value of money in those days if he bears in mind that Wesley's salary was 30 pounds a year.

Once she was temporarily discouraged from buying a building, used as a place of amusement, for a much needed chapel in a suburb of London, because the various ministers whom she consulted felt it would be an impossible undertaking. Said she: "Though at this moment I have not a penny to command, yet I am so firmly persuaded of the goodness of the Master whose I am, and whom I desire to serve, that I shall not want gold or silver for the work. Nevertheless, with some regret, I give up the matter this time; those on the spot may be able to judge better than I can, but *faith* tells me to go forward, nothing fearing, nothing doubting."

Lady Huntingdon having relinquished her plans, the place was bought by another group of worshipers who set up an effective ministry in the neighborhood, visiting the sick, ministering to the needy, and gathering in many souls for Christ's kingdom. This aroused the animosity of the minister of the parish, who determined to drive out the worshipers. He claimed the right to take charge of the chapel himself, insisted that the offerings be turned over to him, and threatened to bring the matter before the ecclesiastical court if his demands were ignored.

When the offending pastors refused to comply with his orders, he summoned them before the consistorial court of the bishop of London, charging them with irregularity in carrying on divine worship in a place not episcopally dedicated and in opposition to the wishes of the minister of the parish. The result was that they were ordered to give up their ministrations. Thus the chapel was closed, and the congregation broken up.

When Lady Huntingdon heard about this, all the ardor of her vigorous nature was aroused. She determined not to let this matter pass unchallenged. Ignoring the timid friends who had kept her from purchasing the chapel in the first place, she sought more daring counselors to help her figure out a way to thwart the efforts of the ministers of the Established Church to repress the preaching of the gospel.

She was advised that if she became proprietor of the chapel it would be placed on a footing with her other chapels and be under the protection and jurisdiction of a peeress of the realm. "Blessed be God," she said, "for the ability and strength which has been given me in the prosecution of this affair."

As her income was only sufficient at this time to take care of the chapels she had already established, she was rebuked by one of her assistants for her rashness in undertaking such a venture. Visiting her at her home, he remonstrated with her over the impropriety of taking on a heavier load than she could possibly bear. While he talked with her, her mail was brought in. As she opened one of the letters, her eyes filled with tears. It said, "An individual who has heard of Lady Huntingdon's exertions to spread the gospel requests her acceptance of the enclosed draft." The draft was for 500 pounds, exactly the amount required to meet the current expenditure. Handing the letter to her visitor, Lady Huntingdon said, "Here, take it, and pay for the chapel; and be no longer faithless, but believing."

The protection that Lady Huntingdon thought she could enjoy as a peeress of the realm did not secure her from persecution. Like Wesley, she was loath to leave the Church of England, but like him and many other earnest believers of the time, she was forced out of the Established Church and compelled to register as a dissenter, thus coming under the protection of the Act of Toleration. "I am to be cast out of the church now," she said, "only for what I have been doing these forty years—speaking and living for Jesus Christ; and if the days of my captivity are now to be accomplished, those that turn me out, and so set me at liberty, may soon feel what it is by sore distress themselves for these hard services which they have caused me. Blessed be the Lord, I have not one care relative to this event, but to be found exactly faithful to God and man through all. I have been severely handled and vilified, but none of these things move me, determined that the short remnant of my life shall be employed in setting up the standard and enlarging the circle of evangelical light and truth.''

In her old age Lady Huntingdon's faith did not dim, nor her courage abate. Her income greatly increased upon the death of her son, but this did not affect her devotion to the principles of self-denial. She allowed herself only one new dress a year, and lived in the sort of simplicity not usually considered adequate for a countess, but quite befitting a child of the King.

"I remember calling on her with a person who came from the country," said a friend of hers. "When we came out he turned his eyes toward the house, and after a short pause exclaimed, 'What a lesson! Can a person of her noble birth, nursed in the lap of grandeur, live in such a house, so meanly furnished? And shall I, a tradesman, be surrounded with luxury and elegance? From this moment I shall hate my house, my furniture, and myself for spending so little for God, and so much in folly.' "

With an income of 1,200 pounds a year, the countess managed to maintain a college at her own expense, erect chapels in various parts of the kingdom, and support preachers in England and America.

Said one of her friends, "Go thou, therefore, who art saying, 'What shall I render unto the Lord for all his benefits?' and do likewise. Thou canst not evidence thy love to God or man by adding house to house and field to field, or by treasuring up thy riches behind the exchange. On the contrary, if God hath given thee wealth with a liberal hand, and thou hast no heart to expend it in His service, it will convince every being but thyself that thou hast no love to Him, and that thy professions are not thy principles.''

Before her death at the age of 84, she was asked by her friend Lady Anne, ''How do you feel?''

''I am well; all is well, well forever,'' she replied. ''I see, wherever I turn my eyes, whether I live or die, nothing but victory.''

Anecdotes

A group of young men were gathered together in a saloon, intent on having some fun mimicking Whitefield and the Wesleys. On a wager, each was to open the Bible at random and speak on the first text that met his eye. Three of them took turns mounting a table and indulging in buffoonery. When the fourth, a 20-year-old youth named John Thorpe, climbed on the table, he stated, "I shall beat you all."

He opened the Bible and read these words: "Except ye repent, ye shall all likewise perish." Immediately he was seized with a conviction of his own sinfulness, and solemnly preached a sermon that was indeed the best of all, for instead of being delivered jestingly it was given with marked earnestness. As he descended from the table, he was greeted with profound silence by his fellow jesters. He left the place never to return to his bacchanalian mummery. Later he became an itinerant preacher, and so he whose mouth formerly poured out foolishness was given the honor of becoming a "fool" for Christ's sake.

Thorpe was not the only young man who set out to mock but became converted instead. One youth climbed a tree during Whitefield's preaching, intent upon ridiculing him. But Whitefield looked up at him and said, "Why don't you imitate Zacchaeus and come down and receive the Lord Jesus?" The question was attended with the power of the Spirit, for the young man heard, obeyed, and believed.

But not all who were convicted were converted. When Whitefield was preaching in London, the most popular comedian in the great city was Edward Shuter, whom Garrick pronounced "the greatest comic genius I ever saw." Shuter went to Whitefield's meetings frequently. The Countess of Huntingdon was so impressed with his interest that she invited him to her home. He told her he could not give up his profession for another more reputable. Writing about him to a friend, she said, "Poor fellow! I think he is not far from the kingdom."

One time when he was at the height of his popularity, he attended a service being conducted at Tottenham Court Chapel, and sat right in front of Whitefield's pulpit. The character the actor was playing at that time was named Ramble. Catching Shuter's eye, Whitefield interrupted his pleadings with the audience to say, "And thou, poor Ramble, who has long rambled from Him, come thou also. Oh, end thy ramblings by coming to Jesus!" Shuter did not resent this personal call, but was almost persuaded. Long after, he told friends who teasingly called him a Methodist, "No, I wish I were; for if any be right, the Methodists are."

Once when traveling with a friend, Whitefield learned that a widow with a large family was about to be evicted from her home because she lacked the money to pay her rent. Never very prosperous himself, Whitefield nonetheless gave the woman the five guineas she needed and in so doing practically emptied his purse. His friend expostulated with him and reminded him that he could ill afford so generous a gift. Whitefield replied, "When God brings a case of distress before us, it is that we may relieve it."

As the two men resumed their journey, they were held up by a highwayman who robbed them of every cent they had. Whitefield—rubbing it in a bit—asked his friend whether it was not much better for the widow to have received his money than for the thief.

Presently the highwayman returned and demanded that Whitefield exchange his good coat for the robber's tattered one. Whitefield did so, not without dismay, and ruefully watched the thief hurry away.

Soon the two travelers noticed that the bandit was again galloping back toward them furiously. This time they determined to take no chances, but to spur their horses on in the hope of reaching a settlement before they were overtaken. They succeeded, and were relieved to find shelter there. When Whitefield took off the disreputable coat forced upon him, he found in one of its pockets a hundred guineas. Thus the Lord is mindful of His own!

When Whitefield went to Boston to preach, he was warmly received by most of the ministers, but jealously regarded by a few. One famous doctor of divinity who happened to meet him on the street said sourly, "I'm sorry to see *you* here!" to which Whitefield replied, "So is the devil."

The devil was not infrequently thwarted in his purposes by the Spirit-filled Whitefield. One time a stonemason, his pocket filled with stones, joined the audience listening to Whitefield, and watched for an opportune moment to throw his stones at the preacher. But the arrows of conviction struck his heart, and the stone in his hand dropped to the ground. After the service was over, he said to Whitefield, "Sir, I came to hear you this day, with a view to break your head; but the Spirit of God, through your ministry, has given me a broken heart." The convicted stonemason became a well-established convert and proved an asset to the cause he once despised.

Dr. Gillies, Whitefield's friend and biographer, tells an interesting story of the conversion of an 18-year-old lad who was celebrating a holiday with a number of his young friends: "The first object that attracted their attention was an old woman, who pretended to tell fortunes. They immediately employed her to tell theirs, and that they might fully qualify her for their undertaking, first made her thoroughly intoxicated with spirituous liquor.

"The young man was informed, among other things, that he would live to a very old age, and see his children, grandchildren, and great-grandchildren growing up around him. Though he had assisted in qualifying the old woman for the fraud, by intoxicating her, yet he had credulity enough to be struck with these parts of her predictions which related to himself.

"'And so,' quoth he, when alone, 'I am to see children, grandchildren, and great-grandchildren! At that age I must be a burden to young people. What shall I do? There is no way for an old man to render himself more agreeable to youth, than by sitting and telling them pleasant and profitable stories. I will, then,' thought he, 'during my youth, endeavour to store my mind with all kinds of knowledge. I will see and hear, and note down everything that is rare and wonderful, that I may sit, when incapable of other employment, and entertain my descendants. Thus shall my company be rendered pleasant, and I shall be respected rather than neglected in old age. Let me see what I can acquire first. Oh! here is the famous Methodist preacher, Whitefield; he is to preach, they say, tonight. I will go and hear him.'

"From these strange motives the young man declared he went to hear Whitefield, who preached that evening from Matthew 3:7: 'But when he saw many of the Pharisees and Sadducees come to his baptism, he said unto them, O generation of vipers, who hath warned you to flee from the wrath to come?' 'Mr. Whitefield,' said the young man, 'described the Sadducean character: this did not touch me. I thought myself as good a Christian as any man in England. From this he went to that of the Pharisees. He described their exterior decency, but observed that the poison of the viper rankled in their hearts. This rather shook me. At length, in the course of his sermon, he abruptly broke off; paused for a few moments; then burst into a flood of tears; lifted up his hands and eyes, and exclaimed, "O my hearers! The wrath's to come! the wrath's to come!"

" 'These words sunk into my heart, like lead in the waters. I wept, and when the sermon was ended, retired alone. For days and weeks I could think of little else. Those awful words would follow me, wherever I went, "The wrath's to come! the wrath's to come!" ' The issue was, that the young man soon after made a public profession of religion, and in a little time became a considerable preacher."

Lord Chesterfield, whose letters to his son, never intended for publication, brought him the fame his other writings failed to achieve, was among those who were fascinated by Whitefield's preaching. One time Whitefield was giving a graphic description of a beggar groping around on the brink of a precipice, over which he stepped. Chesterfield was so moved by Whitefield's oratory that he jumped up and, with an exclamation, cried, "The beggar's gone!"

In one of his letters, Whitefield describes the interesting conversion of a man noted for his wit: "Good Mr. P. told me I should be very shortly favoured with the company of a very pensive and uncommon person—a man of good parts, ready wit, and lively imagination, who, in order to furnish matter for preaching over a bottle, had made it his business to come and hear, and then carry away scraps of my sermons to serve as texts for his tavern harangues.

"A few nights ago, he came, for this purpose, to Dr. Sewall's meeting. Upon my coming in, he crowded after me amongst the people, and having got sufficient matter to work upon, attempted to go out; but, being pent in on every side, his endeavours were fruitless. Obliged thus to stay, waiting for fresh matter for ridicule, he was pricked to the heart. He came to Mr. P., full of horror, confessed his crimes, and longed to ask my pardon, but was afraid to see me. Mr. P. encouraged him to venture.

"This morning, hearing someone knock at my parlour door, I arose, and, upon opening the door, by the paleness, pensiveness, and horror of his countenance, guessed who he was. He cried, 'Sir, can you forgive me?' I smiled, and said, 'Yes, sir, very readily.' He replied, 'Indeed, sir, you cannot when I tell you all.' I then asked him to sit down; and, judging that he had sufficiently felt the lashes of the law, I preached to him the gospel.''

Amazing Manifestations

They seemed like persons awakened by the last trump, and coming out of their graves to judgment," wrote Whitefield when describing the effect of his preaching upon the multitudes.

The amazing manifestations that often occurred at the services held by Whitefield, as well as by John Wesley, have been a source of wonder and perplexity to many. That people wept is not surprising; even tawdry moving pictures often produce that result. But that the audience should groan, and scream, and faint, and sink to the ground convulsively is so unusual that many are at a loss to explain this phenomenon. The coldly critical observer of the twentieth century would put it down to mass hysteria; even the skeptics of the eighteenth century described it in similarly scornful terms. Indeed, some of the Methodists themselves were distressed over these manifestations—Charles Wesley so much so that at one of his meetings he gave warning that no such spectacle was to take place. And none did. But Charles, though a powerful poet, was a dry preacher, and not always were his lips touched with coals from off the altar. He lacked the melting love that so wondrously possessed both John Wesley and Whitefield.

A scornful Philadelphian, writing about the effect of Whitefield's preaching, said: "Field preaching prevails with the vulgar in Philadelphia so much, that industry, honest labour, and care for their families seem to be held, by man, as sinful, and as a mark that they neglect the salvation of their souls. Mr. Whitefield and his adherent ministers have infatuated the multitude with the doctrines of regeneration, free grace, conversion, et cetera, representing them as essential articles of religion, though, in reality, they are inconsistent with true religion, natural and revealed, and are subversive of all order and decency, and repugnant to common sense.

"Every day we have instances of the melancholy fruits of these sermons. Many, of weak minds, are terrified into despair, by the threatenings of eternal vengeance. Some are so transported with the passions which influence them, that they believe they have had the beatific vision, and immediate intercourse with Him who is invisible. . . . Mr. Whitefield is the more to be guarded against, because, I can assure you, he is qualified to sway and keep the affections of the multitude."

Apparently when Whitefield himself first heard of these manifestations at Wesley's meetings, he objected to such demonstrations. Concerning this, Wesley wrote in his journal: "I had an opportunity to talk with Mr. Whitefield of those outward signs which had so often accompanied the inward work of God. I found his objections were chiefly grounded on gross misrepresentations of matter of fact. But the next day, he had an opportunity of informing himself better; for no sooner had he begun, in the application of his sermon, to invite all sinners to believe in Christ, than four persons sunk down close to him, almost in the same moment.

"One of them lay without either sense or motion. A second trembled exceedingly. A third had strong convulsions all over his body, but made no noise, unless by groans. The fourth, equally convulsed, called upon God with strong cries and tears. From this time, I trust, we shall all suffer God to carry on His own work in the way that pleaseth Him.''

At the same time Whitefield wrote: ''That good, great good, is done is evident. Either this is done by an evil or good spirit. If you say by an evil spirit, I answer in our Lord's own words, 'If Satan also be divided against himself, how shall his kingdom stand?' If by a good Spirit, why do not the clergy and the rest of the Pharisees believe our report?

''It is little less than blasphemy against the Holy Ghost to impute the great work, that has been in so short a time wrought in this kingdom, to delusion and the power of the devil.''

A description of the scenes frequently occurring at these meetings is given by Whitefield himself in a letter to a friend. He wrote: ''Most of the people were drowned in tears. The word was sharper than a two-edged sword. The bitter cries and groans were enough to pierce the hardest heart. Some of the people were as pale as death; others were wringing their hands; others lying on the ground; others sinking into the arms of their friends; and most lifting up their eyes to heaven, and crying to God for mercy.''

This occurred in America, but the same phenomena took place in England, where in field or meetinghouse there were often outcries, faintings, and convulsions. Incidentally, similar manifestations occurred in America in the nineteenth century during the great revivals conducted by Charles Finney.

The question naturally arises: What is the explanation of such occurrences? Were they from God or from the devil? Were they the reactions of disordered minds, or the result of the movings of the Spirit? Were they wholesome or unwholesome? Beneficial or harmful?

To find an answer, we turn to that fountain of wisdom, the Bible. Are there records there of faintings or fallings occurring under the conviction of the Spirit? Yes. From the experiences of patriarchs and prophets we learn that there is no terror that can come to human beings more powerful than that produced by an awakening to the corruption of one's own nature. Such a revelation is always brought on by contact with a heavenly being, whose pure and sinless nature contrasts so sharply with man's.

One time Isaiah saw the Lord "high and lifted up" and surrounded by seraphim. His immediate reaction was, "Woe is me! for I am undone; because I am a man of unclean lips, and I dwell in the midst of a people of unclean lips: for mine eyes have seen the King, the Lord of hosts" (Isa. 6:5). Not until he was assured that his iniquity was taken away and his sin purged was the sinking heart of the great gospel prophet revived.

Daniel was similarly affected when he saw the Heavenly Being whose eyes were as lamps of fire: "There remained no strength in me: for my comeliness was turned in me into corruption, and I retained no strength" (Dan. 10:8). Daniel was greatly beloved in heaven, he was a prophet of the Highest, but well he knew that in his humanity he was altogether unworthy to stand before God. But the angel Gabriel touched him and bade him to stand upright, and said to the trembling prophet, "Fear not" (verse 12).

Paul fell to the earth and was blinded when he caught a glimpse of the Lord Jesus. He too trembled, and with astonishment asked, "Lord, what wilt thou have me to do?" (Acts 9:6).

The first great work of the Holy Spirit is to reprove the world of sin, and that always causes one's face to gather paleness and one's heart to faint. A minister once urged his flock *never* to ask the Lord to reveal to them the utter corruption of their hearts unless they were prepared to take the consequences. He said he himself made such a prayer one time, and after it was answered he was unable to preach for a year.

It must ever be borne in mind that whenever the Lord does a great work, the devil is quick to follow with a counterfeit. If the Lord smites men down with a powerful conviction of their sinfulness, the devil finds it easy to imitate this by producing hysterical spectacles designed to cast reproach upon the true manifestations of the Spirit. This undoubtedly sometimes occurred during the Methodist revivals of the eighteenth century. Both Wesley and Whitefield recognized such a possibility. The latter said the sudden agonies and roarings of the people proceeded generally from soul distress, but sometimes, possibly, from the agency of evil spirits laboring to drive poor souls into despair.

At one time when Wesley was holding meetings in Newcastle, there was much excitement. A number of people fell down and went through agonizing experiences. Some complained that they felt a great weight upon their chests and could hardly breathe; others said it seemed as if a sword were thrust through them. Still others felt as if they were being torn to pieces. "These symptoms I can no more impute to any natural causes, than to the Spirit of God," said Wesley. "I can make no doubt, but it was Satan tearing them, as they were coming to Christ. And hence proceeded those grievous cries, whereby he might design both to discredit the work of God, and to affright fearful people from hearing that word whereby their souls might be saved."

But these apparently satanic manifestations were the exception rather than the rule at the meetings of Whitefield and Wesley. There is no doubt that usually the groaning and fainting occurred as a result of hearts being mightily and marvelously moved by the Holy Spirit.

There is good reason for so believing. The Lord Jesus has given us a test to apply to every man's work so that we need not be in ignorance as to its worth: "By their fruits ye shall know them" (Matt. 7:20). What were the fruits of Whitefield's work? What was the aftermath of meetings at which these strange manifestations took place? I am not referring to the fruit—so eminently good—of his entire lifework, but specifically to the results of his preaching when it was attended by these remarkable exhibitions. Let us take as only one example a letter written in the New England *Journal* at a time when there was much fainting and crying at Whitefield's meetings:

"The alteration in the face of religion in Philadelphia is surprising. Never did the people shew so great a willingness to attend sermons, nor the preachers greater zeal and diligence in performing the duties of their function. Religion has become the subject of most conversations. No books are in request, but those of piety and devotion. Instead of singing idle songs and ballads, the people are everywhere entertaining themselves with psalms and hymns and spiritual songs. All this, under God, is owing to the successful labours of the Reverend Mr. Whitefield."

These were the happy results in the lives of a people who were first wounded and then healed by Him who "healeth the broken in heart, and bindeth up their wounds" (Ps. 147:3), for assuredly "the sacrifices of God are a broken spirit: a broken and a contrite heart, O God, thou wilt not despise" (chap. 51:17).

It is not stretching the point to emphasize, as has been pointed out by others, that the revivals brought through the instrumentality of Wesley and Whitefield prevented a revolution in England similar to the dread-fully devastating French Revolution. Conditions in England at the opening of the eighteenth century were ripe for just such a cataclysmic upheaval, but, thanks to the indefatigable labors of the Spirit-filled Wesleys and Whitefield, the nation was spared that catastrophe.

Whitefield and the Wesleys

I could scarce reconcile myself at first to this strange way of preaching in the fields; having been all my life, till very lately, so tenacious of every point relating to decency and order, that I should have thought the saving of souls almost a sin if it had not been done in a church,'' said John Wesley concerning his first outdoor preaching venture. It was Whitefield who paved the way for the field preaching that became so characteristic of the ministry of the Methodists.

"Yesterday I began to play the madman in Gloucestershire, by preaching on a table in Thornbury Street," Whitefield had written to John, urging him to follow his example. John reluctantly agreed, and thus commenced that marvelous career of preaching in the streets and fields all over Great Britain. Dignified and scholarly man that he was, Wesley never liked that method—it was always irksome to him. He said, "What marvel the devil does not love field preaching! Neither do I. I love a commodious room, a soft cushion, and a handsome pulpit. But where is my zeal, if I do not trample all these under foot, in order to save one more soul!" He never got quite used to field preaching. When he was nearly 70 he remarked, "To this day field preaching is a cross to me; but I know my commission, and see no other way of preaching the gospel to every creature."

It must have taken a lot of pride-swallowing for Wesley to stand up in a crowded marketplace and, after gathering a gaping crowd about him by singing a hymn, to say, "If you wish to know who I am, my name is John Wesley, and I have come here to preach the gospel!"

Whitefield was delighted that John had followed his example, and would not rest content untill Charles did likewise. There was a little streak of snobbishness in the formal, High-Church Charles, and his nature must indeed have recoiled at the thought of taking such a step, but, soon after, he "broke down the bridge, became desperate," and "cried to multitudes upon multitudes, 'Repent ye, and believe the gospel!'" He said the Lord was his strength, his mouth, and his wisdom.

The affection that existed between the three young Methodist preachers was so close, so warm, and so beautiful that often they took sweet counsel together and encouraged one another through the trials and persecutions that attended their early ministry.

Whitefield's friendship was particularly needed when John went through the heartbreaking experience of having his engagement to Grace Murray broken by the interference of his brother, Charles. John had announced his intention of marrying Grace, to the dismay of Charles, who thought her far beneath his brother's dignity and spoke of her as a servant girl. So intent was Charles on breaking up the match that, during John's absence, he persuaded the somewhat fickle but charming woman to marry John Bennet, who was very much in love with her. John Wesley's pathetic account of his reaction to the news of Grace's marriage follows:

"At Leeds, I found, not my brother, but Mr. Whitefield. I lay down by him on the bed. He told me my brother would not come till John Bennet and Grace Murray were married. I was troubled; he perceived it; he wept and prayed over me, but I could not shed a tear. He said all that was in his power to comfort me, but it was in vain.

"He told me it was his judgment that she was *my* wife, and that he had said so to John Bennet, that he would fain have persuaded them to wait, and not to marry till they had seen me; but that my brother's impetuosity prevailed and bore down all before it.

"On Thursday, October 5, about eight, one came in from Newcastle, and told us, 'They were married on Tuesday.' My brother came an hour after. I felt no anger, yet I did not desire to see him; but Mr. Whitefield constrained me.

"After a few words had passed, he accosted me with, 'I renounce all intercourse with you, but what I would have with a heathen man or a publican.' I felt little emotion; it was only adding a drop of water to a drowning man; yet I calmly accepted his renunciation, and acquiesced therein. Poor Mr. Whitefield and John Nelson burst into tears. They prayed, cried, and entreated, till the storm passed away. We could not speak, but only fell on each other's neck."

John and Charles were completely reconciled and worked together lovingly and devotedly during the long years that followed.

The friendship between Whitefield and the Wesleys was the sort that Satan particularly likes to break up, and he watched for an opportunity to do so to bring reproach on their great work for God. That opportunity came, and for a time a shadow was cast over the lives of the young men.

Often the three discussed the Reformation of the sixteenth century, which was of particular interest to them because they were raised up to do a work of reform also. All three reacted alike to the tragic mistakes the

Reformers made, particularly Luther in his controversy with Zwingli over the question of the Lord's Supper. Whitefield and the Wesleys were saddened to read of Luther's refusal to shake hands with Zwingli because the latter would not accept his interpretation of the expression "This is my body." All three were determined that no matter what happened, they would not similarly fail to maintain Christian love.

When Whitefield visited America, his contacts with the Presbyterians aroused his interest in the formidable subject of predestination, and he began to favor it heartily. Convinced that only those were saved who were elected and predestined for salvation by God, he became so enthusiastic over the doctrine that he determined to bring the Wesleys to his viewpoint also. In this he was unsuccessful.

Recalling the controversy between Luther and Zwingli, Whitefield wrote to John Wesley in the spirit we would expect him to show, "Let this, dear sir, be a caution to us; I hope it will to me; for, by the blessing of God, provoke me to it as much as you please, I do not think ever to enter the lists of controversy with you on the points wherein we differ."

Wesley replied in an equally Christian spirit: "The case is quite plain. There are bigots both for predestination and against it. God is sending a message to those on either side, but neither will receive it unless from one who is of their own opinion. Therefore, for a time you are suffered to be of one opinion, and I of another. But when His time is come, God will do what men cannot, namely, make us both of one mind."

Both men would willingly have avoided entering into any public controversy with each other. However, they were virtually forced into it by the immense agitation that took place in England when some of the Calvinists became vitriolic in their pamphlets and discussions on the subject.

Led away from his usual forbearance by his excessive zeal, the youthful Whitefield (about 25 years old at this time) wrote a pamphlet in a sharp spirit. One of Wesley's friends urged him to reply to it, but he said, "You may read Whitefield against Wesley; but you shall never read Wesley against Whitefield."

Wesley did, however, preach a powerful sermon on free grace that irked Whitefield very much, for it presented the doctrine of predestination in a most unappealing light.

During the tense period of disagreement, there was even a certain amount of distrust between the two men, for "friends" of both endeavored to add fuel to the fire. At this time Charles wrote Whitefield a beautiful letter designed to make peace. He said:

"My brother has been most grossly abused; his behavior (if I may be a witness) has been truly Christian. All the bitterness his opposers have shewn, and the woes and curses they have denounced against him, have never provoked him to a like return, or stirred his temper, or impaired his charity; much less are we cooled in our affection towards you, by all the idle stories we hear of your opposition to us.

"Your zealous, indiscreet friends, instead of concealing any little difference between us, have told it in Gath, and published it in Askelon; but I trust, by our first meeting, all will know that those things whereof they were informed concerning us are nothing, while we stand fast in one mind and in one spirit, striving together for the faith of the gospel. This is of the last importance to the cause we maintain, which suffered so much, as you well observe, by the dissensions of the first Reformers.

"Oh, my friend, if you have the glory of God and the

salvation of souls at heart, resolve, by the Divine grace, that nothing upon earth, nor under the earth, shall part us. God increase the horror He has given me of a separation! I had rather you saw me dead at your feet than openly opposing you. . . .

"Many, I know, desire nothing so much as to see George Whitefield and John Wesley at the head of different parties, as is plain from their truly devilish plans to effect it; but be assured, my dearest brother, our heart is as your heart. Oh, may we always thus continue to think and speak the same things! When God has taught us mutual forbearance, long-suffering and love, who knows but He may bring us into an exact agreement in all things? In the meantime, I do not think the difference is considerable.

"I shall never dispute with you touching election; and, if you know not yet to reconcile that doctrine with God's universal love, I will cry unto Him, 'Lord, what we know not, shew Thou us!' but never offend you by my different sentiment. My soul is set upon peace, and drawn after you by love stronger than death. You know not how dear you are to me; not dearer, I will be bold to say, to any of your natural or spiritual relations.

"Charles Wesley"

Charles understood that "now we see through a glass, darkly; but then face to face:" and that now we know in part (or imperfectly), but then shall we know even as also we are known (1 Cor. 13:12).

There were other subjects besides predestination on which Whitefield and John Wesley disagreed, but as one studies their viewpoints, it would seem that they were like two men looking at a large building, one standing at the southeast corner and the other at the northwest, each describing what he saw. They were simply talking about different aspects of the subjects, but actually on the most important aspects they were agreed, though they could not at first see it.

In their disagreements, it was Whitefield who conducted himself more rashly than Wesley, who never forgot his responsibility as a spiritual father. His attitude toward Whitefield, as he himself put it, was "Spare the young man, even Absalom, for my sake."

Under such circumstances, the breach between the good friends could not last long. The Lord Himself took a hand in humbling the too-impetuous young man. When Whitefield returned to England, his audiences dwindled, his popularity waned. He acknowledged the humiliating experience himself:

"Once, at Kennington Common, I had not above a hundred to hear me. . . . For some time, I continued to preach twice a day under one of the trees, and had the mortification of seeing numbers of my spiritual children, who but a twelvemonth ago would have plucked out their eyes for me, running by me whilst preaching, disdaining so much as to look at me; and some of them putting their fingers in their ears, that they might not hear one word I said. . . . Busybodies, on both sides, blew up the coals. . . . A breach ensued. But, as both sides differed in judgment, and not in affection, and aimed at the glory of our common Lord (though on both sides we hearkened too much to talebearers), we were kept from anathematizing each other, and went on in our usual way; being agreed in one point, endeavouring to convert souls to the ever-blessed Mediator."

One of Whitefield's outstanding and lovable characteristics was a willingness to admit his faults. He wrote: "Alas, alas! In how many things have I judged and acted wrong! I have been too rash and hasty in giving characters, both of places and persons. Being fond of Scripture language, I have often used a style too apostolical; and, at the same time, I have been too bitter in my zeal.

"Wildfire has been mixed with it; and I frequently wrote and spoke in my own spirit, when I thought I was writing and speaking by the assistance of the Spirit of God. . . . By these things I have hurt the blessed cause I would defend, and have stirred up needless opposition.

"At the same time, I cannot but bless and praise that good and gracious God, who filled me with so much of His holy fire, and carried me, a poor weak youth, through such a torrent both of popularity and contempt, and set so many seals to my unworthy ministration. I bless Him for ripening my judgment a little more, and for giving me to see and confess, and, I hope, in some degree, to correct and amend, some of my mistakes."

Lovingly he wrote to the Wesleys:

"This is the language of my heart:

'O let us find the ancient way,
        Our wondering foes to move;
And force the heathen world to say,
        See how these Christians love.'

"I purpose to be in London in a few days. Meanwhile, I salute you and all the followers of the blessed Lamb of God most heartily."

In later years, John Wesley wrote: "In every place where Mr. Whitefield has been, he has laboured in the same friendly, Christian manner. God has indeed effectually broken down the wall of partition which was between us. Thirty years ago we were one; then the sower of tares rent us asunder; but now a stronger than he has made us one again."

Personal Habits

B e not slothful in business. Go to bed seasonably, and rise early. Redeem your precious time. Pick up all the fragments of it, that not one moment may be lost," wrote Whitefield to a friend. And in a sermon the preacher said, "God convert you from lying abed in the morning!"

He followed his own advice. It was his custom to arise at four or five o'clock every morning, and to keep active until ten at night. Often he preached at six or seven in the morning, and conducted personal interviews an hour before. It is said that he never preached greater sermons than at six in the morning. In this respect he was like Wesley, who preached even earlier, at five, and sometimes even at four!

Not without reason were Whitefield and the Wesleys dubbed Methodists, for they were certainly methodical about everything they did. Time was a precious talent of which they were stewards, and every moment had to be properly utilized.

When Whitefield was at home, meals had to be served on the dot. "A few minutes' delay would be considered a great fault," writes Cornelius Winter, a youth who lived with him during the last two years of his life. "He was irritable, but soon appeased. Not being patient enough, one day, to receive a reason for his being disappointed, he hurt the mind of one who was studious to please; but, on reflection, he burst into tears, saying, 'I shall live to be a poor peevish old man, and everybody will be tired of me.'"

Although his meals were very simple, the table had to be spread elegantly. Sometimes it was graced only with a cowheel, one of his favorite dishes. "How surprised would the world be, if they were to peep upon Dr. Squintum, and see a cowheel only upon his table," he once remarked. (He had been nicknamed Dr. Squintum by a comedian because of a squint in one of his eyes, an aftermath of the measles.)

If Whitefield was meticulous about his meals, he was even more so about his apparel. He smilingly said, "A minister of the gospel ought to be without spot." When he was first spiritually awakened as a teen-ager, however, he thought it was a sign of proper humility to dress shabbily. "My apparel was mean," he wrote in his journal. "I thought it unbecoming a penitent to have his hair powdered. I wore woollen gloves, a patched gown, and dirty shoes." But soon he took a well-balanced attitude toward the subject of dress, and followed his natural bent for neatness. To a friend who reproached him for being too "decent" in appearance, he wrote: "I could not but smile, to find you wink at the *decency of my dress.* Alas! my brother, I have long since known what it is to be in that state, into which I fear you are about to enter. I once thought that Christianity required me to go nasty. I neglected myself as much as you would have me, for about a twelvemonth; but, when God gave me the spirit of adoption, I then dressed *decently,* as you call it, out of principle; and I am more and more convinced, that the Lord would have me act, in that respect, as I do."

Unlike Wesley, who refused to fall in with the custom of the times by wearing a wig (to the despair of his friends and relatives), Whitefield always wore one. One time when he was preaching in Moorfields, he almost lost it. A young man attempted to stab him in the temple, and in so doing disturbed his hat and wig. The evangelist would undoubtedly have been killed if a bystander had not interfered by striking the sword with his cane.

A passion for neatness so possessed Whitefield that Cornelius Winter said, "Not a paper must be out of place, or be put up irregularly. Each part of the furniture, likewise, must be in its proper position before we retired to rest. He said he did not think he should die easy, if he thought his gloves were not where they ought to be."

He was just as meticulous in regard to financial obligations, and would not have approved of the popular custom so much in vogue today: installment buying. He did not purchase anything until he had the money to pay for it on the spot. He went beyond being merely scrupulously honest in handling money, he was generous and largehearted in dispensing it.

His honesty showed itself in another quality more rarely found and therefore more heartily appreciated: his refreshing candor. Wesley called attention to this in his sermon at Whitefield's funeral. He said, "The *frankness and openness* of his conversation was as far removed from rudeness on the one hand, as from guile and disguise on the other. Was not this frankness at once a fruit and a proof of his *courage* and *intrepidity?* Armed with these, he feared not the faces of men, but used *great plainness of speech* to persons of every rank and condition, high and low, rich and poor; endeavouring only by *manifestation of the truth to commend himself to every man's conscience in the sight of God.*"

Such candor and courage could only be found in a man whose motivation was pure. He said that as long as the secret of the Lord was with him, he cared not if there was a window in his heart for all mankind to see the uprightness of his intentions. There was a simplicity and artlessness about Whitefield that brought upon him much criticism and persecution, but nevertheless drew honest hearts to him.

And the secret of his ingenuous, unworldly character was found in the hours he spent in prayer. When he was a mere youth of 22, he wrote in his journal: "I had a sweet knot of religious friends. . . . Once we spent a whole night in prayer and praise; and many a time, at midnight and at one in the morning, after I had been wearied almost to death in preaching, writing, and conversation, and going from place to place, God imparted new life to my soul, and enabled me to intercede with Him for an hour and a half and two hours together."

Whitefield felt that if one wanted to keep up the walk with God, he must pray without ceasing. "O prayer, prayer!" he said in one of his impassioned sermons, "it brings and keeps God and man together; it raises man up to God, and brings God down to man. . . . When you are about the common business of life, be much in ejaculatory prayer. Send, from time to time, short letters post to heaven, upon the wings of faith. They will reach the very heart of God, and will return to you with blessings."

Though others may have viewed him as a great saint, Whitefield knew himself to be merely a sinner being saved by grace, a "hell-deserving but redeemed creature," as he put it. He longed to be a blank in the hands of Jesus. In withering terms he described that monster *self*, meaning himself: "O for further leadings into the chambers of that selfish, sensual, and devilish imagery, that yet lie latent in my partly renewed heart! This self-love, what a *Proteus!* This self-will, what a *Hydra!* This remaining body of sin and death, what an *Antichrist!* what a scarlet whore! what a hell! what a red dragon! what a cursed monster is it! How hard, how slow, he dies!''

He understood clearly that the work of sanctification was the work of a lifetime, and a task that must be accomplished by the Holy Spirit. In describing his dealings with sin in himself, he wrote to a titled Scotch lady: "The Lord empties before He fills; humbles before He exalts. At least, He is pleased to deal thus with me. I thank Him for it, from my inmost soul; for were it not so, His mercies would destroy us. When I discover a new corruption, I am as thankful as a sentinel, keeping watch in a garrison, would be at spying a straggling enemy come near him.

"I stand not fighting with it in my own strength, but run immediately and tell the Captain of my salvation. By the sword of the Spirit, He soon destroys it. This is what I call a simple looking to Christ. I know of no other effectual way of keeping the old man down. Look up then, dear madam, to a wounded Saviour. Tell Him your whole heart. Go to Him as a little child. He will hear your lisping, and set your soul at liberty."

That such a method of meeting sin from within really worked is attested by a statement Whitefield wrote in one of his letters: "Thanks be to His great name; I can truly say, that, for many years past, no sin has had dominion over me; neither have I slept with the guilt of any known, unrepented sin lying upon my heart."

The great preacher had such a blessed assurance of salvation that he had no fear of death, and indeed actually longed for death. This is not to be wondered at when one considers the fearful amount of opposition and persecution he continually endured. He was never without some opponent whose one object seemed to be to make his life miserable. He was continually being made an "offender for a word." His longing for death may also have been caused by his frequent illnesses.

At any rate, he was one time taken to task by a fellow minister for so often manifesting a desire to die. This happened at a dinner attended by a group of ministers. Whitefield expressed himself as being wearied by the burdens of the day and finding consolation in the fact that he would soon be going to rest. He asked the other ministers whether they did not feel the same way, and most of them assented. Mr. Tennent, however, remained silent. Noticing this, Whitefield tapped him on the knee and said, "Well! Brother Tennent, you are the oldest man amongst us; do you not rejoice to think that your time is so near at hand, when you will be called home?"

Mr. Tennent answered, "I have no wish about it." But Whitefield pressed him again, determined to get him to agree. At this, Mr. Tennent replied, "No, sir, it is no pleasure to me at all; and if you knew your duty, it would be none to you. I have nothing to do with death; my business is to live as long as I can, as well as I can, and to serve my Master as faithfully as I can, until He shall think proper to call me home."

Whitefield asked what his attitude would be if he had his own choice in the matter. Said Mr. Tennent, "I have no choice about it: I am God's servant, and have engaged to do His business as long as He pleases to continue me therein. But now, brother, let me ask you a question. What do you think I would say, if I was to send my man Tom into the field to plough; and if at noon I should go to the field, and find him lounging under a tree, and complaining, 'Master, the sun is very hot, and the ploughing very hard; I am weary of the work you have appointed me, and am overdone with the heat and burden of the day: do master, let me return home, and be discharged from this hard service'? What would I say? Why, that he was a lazy fellow; that it was his business to do the work

I had appointed him, until I should think it fit to call him home." That answer quieted Whitefield.

The one thing he dreaded supremely was the thought of outliving his usefulness. He wanted ever to minister rather than to be ministered unto. "O that death may find me either praying or preaching!" he said.

In a letter to a friend, he wrote of Lady Huntingdon's sister-in-law, who had just died. "She was a retired Christian [who] lived silently, and died suddenly, without a groan. May my exit be like hers! Whether right or not, I cannot help wishing that I may go off in the same manner. To me it is worse than death to live to be nursed, and see friends weeping about one. Sudden death is sudden glory. But all this must be left to our heavenly Father."

God graciously fulfilled Whitefield's wish, and he died just the way he wanted to, suddenly, the morning after delivering a two-hour sermon.

Attitude Toward Money

Simple-hearted Christian that he was, Whitefield had a childlike attitude toward money, based on the great promises of God. Whitefield loved the text "Seek ye first the kingdom of God, and his righteousness; and all these things shall be added unto you" (Matt. 6:33), and purposed throughout life to take God at His word. In so doing, he was following in the footsteps of that remarkable German scholar and saint Professor August Hermann Francke, whose amazing faith-work in the care of orphans has been a shining beacon light to his successors. Whitefield wrote in his journal: "For some considerable time, I had followed the example of Professor Frank [*sic*], and, whenever I wanted any worldly assistance, pleaded the Scripture promises for the things of this life, as well as that which is to come, in the name of Jesus Christ. This is still my practice, and I never yet failed of success."

Whitefield tells how when he was especially pressed for money for the necessities of life, he would tell his troubles to the Lord, who brought assistance in the most unexpected ways and from the most surprising sources. "Those I expected should assist me did not; but persons I never spoke to, and who, I thought, were my enemies, were raised up to supply my wants."

One time Whitefield and a friend of his visited a

wealthy family that they knew delighted to do good. "It being my constant practice to improve my acquaintance with the rich for the benefit of the poor, I recommended two poor clergymen, and another pious person, to their charity," Whitefield wrote. They generously gave him about thity-six guineas for these needy workers. Later the friend who accompanied Whitefield remarked, "If you had not spoken for others, you would have had a good deal of that yourself." But the young preacher, penniless at the time, had no regrets, for he knew his rich Father had far more wealth than the wealthiest of men. When his mail was delivered the next day, he found a ten-pound note in the first letter he opened. It was from a wholly unexpected source.

Unlike a modern popular minister who boasts that he always travels first class because he is the representative of a great King, Whitefield practiced self-denial and was careful to hold to a minimum his expenditures for personal needs. If he hired a house it was at "a very cheap rate"; when he ate a meal it was "a morsel of bread, and a little bit of cold meat," and this he considered "a most luxurious repast." "Ceiled houses and crowded tables I leave to others," he wrote. It was his desire to go without purse or scrip, letting the Master bear his charges.

"Mr. W. wishes there may be a contribution for myself," he wrote to a friend, "but I will not admit of any such thing. I make no purse. What I have, I give away. Freely I have received; freely I desire to give. 'Poor, yet making many rich,' shall be my motto still."

After his marriage, he received the loan of some furniture for his house, and brought his wife "a second-hand suit of curtains" for their humble dwelling place. This little house in Abergavenny, Wales, was very dear to him. One time when he spent forty-eight hours resting there after a strenuous tour, he spoke of his "sweet, very sweet retirement—so sweet that I should be glad never to be heard of again. But this must not be. A necessity is laid upon me; and woe is me, if I preach not the gospel of Christ."

Whitefield, like John Wesley and George Mueller, took very literally the counsel Christ gave in the Sermon on the Mount: "Lay not up for yourselves treasures upon earth, where moth and rust doth corrupt, and where thieves break through and steal: but lay up for yourselves treasures in heaven, where neither moth nor rust doth corrupt, and where thieves do not break through nor steal: for where your treasure is, there will your heart be also" (verses 19-21).

While accused of using the vast sums he collected for his orphanage in Georgia for self-aggrandizement, Whitefield was actually very poor, having no fixed income. Yet it was publicly and officially attested that out of his own purse he had given more than 3,000 pounds for orphans, a huge amount when one considers the value of money in those days. The gifts he had received for personal use were indeed laid up in the bank of heaven, where he had counseled others to put their treasure.

"My dear sir," he wrote to one of his correspondents, "let us be laudably ambitious to get as rich as we can towards God. The bank of heaven is a sure bank. I have drawn thousands of bills upon it, and never had one sent back protested. God helping me, I purpose lodging my little earthly all there. I hope my present poor but valuable cargo will make some additions to my heavenly inheritance."

Throughout his ministry, Whitefield was careful not to cater to those who wanted their ministers to speak unto them smooth things and prophesy deceits. Like

Wesley, he was especially outspoken on the subject of covetousness, for he knew that indeed "the love of money is the root of all evil" (1 Tim. 6:10). He wrote plainly to a wealthy miser: "Your friends everywhere take notice, that the sin which doth most easily beset you is a too great love of money; and this, in many cases, makes you act an unfriendly part. If God should suffer our enemies to prevail, you will wish you had laid up more treasure in heaven. Blessed be God, mine is out of the reach of men or devils. Strange that 5 percent from man should be preferred to a hundredfold from Christ! A word to the wise is sufficient."

Whitefield followed his own advice. One time when he was visiting the flock with his friend Kinsman, he gave money, as well as counsel, to those who needed it. On the way home Kinsman cautioned him about his excessive generosity, reminding him that his own finances were low. "Young man," answered Whitefield, "it is not enough to pray, and to put on a serious countenance: 'Pure religion and undefiled . . . is this, To visit the fatherless and widows in their affliction,' and to administer to their wants. My stock, I grant, is nearly exhausted, but God will soon send me a fresh supply."

In the evening a man called and asked to see Whitefield. "Sir," said he, "I heard you preach yesterday: you are on a journey, as well as myself; and, as traveling is expensive, will you do me the honour of accepting this?" That the present offered was five guineas was surprising enough, but that it came from a man noted for his penuriousness was all the more astonishing.

"Young man," said Whitefield when next he spoke to Kinsman, "God has soon repaid what I bestowed. Learn, in future, not to withhold when it is in the power of your hand to give."

Despising the attitude of those who wanted to cling to earthly treasures, Whitefield once announced after his sermon, "We shall sing a hymn, during which those who do not choose to give their mite may sneak off." Of course, not one person in the audience stirred. The preacher then ordered all the doors locked except one; he himself stood at that one, holding the plate as the congregation walked out. Doubtless he forgot on that occasion that the Lord loves *cheerful* givers, and that those who give through compulsion will be rewarded only in proportion to the spirit that accompanies the gift.

Before his last trip to America, Whitefield preached in the Tottenham Court Road chapel. To the crowd gathered to hear him he said: "I am going trusting in God to bear my charges. I call heaven and earth to witness that I have never had the love of the world one quarter of an hour in my heart. I might have been rich; but now, though this chapel is built, and though I have a comfortable room to live in, I assure you I built the room at my own expense. It cost nobody but myself anything, and I shall leave it with an easy mind. . . . I might have had a thousand a year out of this place, if I had chosen it. When I am gone to heaven, you will see what I have got on earth. I do not like to speak now, because it might be thought boasting."

It is fascinating to notice that, though Whitefield was poor all his life because of his generosity, and made no attempt to set aside a little nest egg for his old age, he nevertheless died in so prosperous a state that he was enabled to leave generous benefactions to his loved ones and friends. This came about because of certain legacies bequeathed to him shortly before his death. It was as if the wealthy Father, to whom he so faithfully gave in the person of His poor, wished him to have that same pleasure in the last days of his life. Thus the poor preacher who had always taught and believed that it was "more blessed to give than to receive" had the joy of leaving 1,400 pounds to relatives and associates who he knew would make good use of the benefaction.

George Whitefield had chosen to be poor in this world but rich in faith, and God added His blessing so that he died rich in this world, as well as in the next.

The Death of Whitefield

Whitefield never returned from his seventh trip to America. For years he had been troubled with physical infirmities and often was so sick that his friends despaired of his life. He tells how he submitted to their wishes when they urged him to rest: "I have omitted preaching one night to oblige my friends, that they may not charge me with murdering myself; but I hope yet to die in the pulpit, or soon after I come out of it."

Again he wrote, "I have been several times on the verge of eternity. At present I am so weak that I cannot preach. It is hard work to be silent, but I must be tried every way."

For years he continued valiantly, rarely letting sickness hinder him in carrying the immense burdens he so bravely bore. Often he referred in his letters to the return of his old trouble—vomiting blood—but always he looked upon preaching and itinerating as the cures for all his ills.

His body was steadily growing weaker, but his spirit was indomitable. On September 29, 1770, one day before his death, he set out from Portsmouth to Boston, intending to preach at Newburyport the next morning. While passing through Exeter, he was asked to preach the sermon that turned out to be his last.

"Sir," remarked a friend to him, "you are more fit to

go to bed than you are to preach."

"True, sir," Whitefield replied, and then looking heavenward, he said, "Lord Jesus, I am weary *in* Thy work, but not *of* it. If I have not yet finished my course, let me go and speak for Thee once more in the fields, seal Thy truth, and come home and die!"

There in a New England field, the dying man preached a sermon on the subject that had always been so dear to him: salvation by faith. One who heard him described his last effort: "The subject was 'Faith and Works.' He rose up sluggishly and wearily, as if worn down and exhausted by his stupendous labours. His face seemed bloated, his voice was hoarse, his enunciation heavy. Sentence after sentence was thrown off in rough, disjointed portions, without much regard to point or beauty.

"At length, his mind kindled, and his lion-like voice roared to the extremities of his audience. He was speaking of the inefficiency of works to merit salvation, and suddenly cried out in a tone of thunder, 'Works! works! a man get to heaven by works! I would as soon think of climbing to the moon on a rope of sand!' "

Another hearer reported that, after being unable to speak for several minutes, he received power to preach perhaps the best of his sermons, closing with the words, "My body fails, my spirit expands. How willingly would I live forever to preach Christ! But I die to be *with* Him."

After the sermon, Whitefield dined at a Captain Gillman's and then continued his journey to Newburyport. There, at a manse connected with a meetinghouse where he had preached thirty years before, he retired after standing on the stairs and giving a few final words of exhortation to the crowd assembled in the hall. Tearfully they gazed at him whom they looked upon as an ascending Elijah. He spoke to them until the candle he was holding flickered out in its socket.

His friend Mr. Richard Smith, who had accompanied him from England and was his constant companion, went into his room and found him reading the Bible, with Dr. Watts's *Psalms of David* lying before him. "My asthma is returning," said Whitefield. "Two or three days' riding, without preaching, will set me up again."

Later he said, "I cannot breathe; but I hope I shall be better by and by; a good pulpit sweat today may give me relief: I shall be better after preaching." Smith said he wished he would not preach so often. He replied, "I had rather wear out than rust out."

Whitefield had always prayed that he would never outlive his usefulness, for he had always wanted to minister rather than to be ministered unto. His prayer was answered, for after a restless night, during which his friends worked over him unsuccessfully, he gasped, stretched out, and died.

In those days people attached much significance to a man's last words. This was a foolish attitude to take, for obviously a dying man is necessarily weakened both physically and mentally. What really matters is the sort of testimony his life has given, not what he may manage to gasp with his last breath.

This was the attitude Whitefield took. Some years before his death, Dr. Finley, the president of Princeton, said to him, "Mr. Whitefield, I hope it will be very long before you will be called home, but when that event shall arrive, I should be glad to hear the noble testimony you will bear for God."

"You would be disappointed, doctor," Whitefield replied prophetically. "I shall die silent. It has pleased God to enable me to bear so many testimonies for Him during my life, that He will require none from me when I die." And thus it was, for he breathed his last breath without uttering any significant last words.

When Whitefield was buried, all the bells in Newburyport were tolled, and the ships in the harbor hoisted mourning signals. The funeral procession was a mile in length. "About 6,000 persons crowded within the church, and many thousands stood outside. The corpse being placed at the foot of the pulpit, the Reverend Daniel Rogers offered prayer, in which he confessed that he owed his conversion to Whitefield's ministry, and then exclaiming, 'O my Father! my Father!' stopped and wept as though his heart was breaking. The scene was one never to be forgotten. The crowded congregation were bathed in tears. Rogers recovered himself, finished his prayer, sat down, and sobbed. One of the deacons gave out the hymn beginning with the line 'Why do we mourn departing friends?' Some of the people sang, and some wept, and others sang and wept alternately. The coffin was then put into a newly prepared tomb, beneath the pulpit; and, before the tomb was sealed, the Reverend Jedediah Jewet delivered a suitable address, in the course of which he spoke of Whitefield's 'peculiar and eminent gifts for the gospel ministry, and his fervour, diligence, and succes in the work of it.' "

Whitefield's death led to the conversion of a young man who had heard him preach two days before, but who had reviled him in his heart. As Benjamin Randall heard a man crying through the streets, "Whitefield is dead! Whitefield is dead!" his heart was pierced. He said to himself, "Whitefield is now in heaven, but I am on the road to hell. He was a man of God, and yet I reviled him. He taught me the way to heaven, but I regarded it not. O that I could hear his voice again!" This youth was soon converted and became the founder of the Free Will Baptist denomination, one that soon grew so large that it had a thousand ministers.

Five weeks later, news of Whitefield's death reached London. Long before, he had requested that John Wesley preach his funeral sermon. Describing the occasion in his journal, Wesley wrote, "The time appointed for my beginning at the Tabernacle was half an hour after five; but it was quite filled at three; so I began at four."

John Wesley, old and tried friend whom Whitefield had called his father in Christ, was well fitted to preach on this solemn occasion. In beautiful tribute to his friend, he chose as his text, "Let me die the death of the righteous, and let my last end be like his!" (Num. 23:10). After reviewing the conversion and the great work of Whitefield, Wesley summarized the doctrines he preached:

"His fundamental point was, 'Give God all the glory of whatever is good in man'; and, 'In the business of salvation, set Christ as high and man as low as possible.' With this point, he and his friends at Oxford, the original Methodists, so called, set out.

"Their grand principle was, There is *no power* (by nature) and *no merit* in man. They insisted, all power to think, speak, or act aright, is in and from the Spirit of Christ; and all merit is (not in man, how high soever in grace, but merely) in the blood of Christ.

"So he and they taught: there is no power in man, till it is given him from above, to do one good work, to speak one good word, or to form one good desire. For it is not enough to say, all men are *sick of sin:* no, we are all '*dead* in trespasses and sins.' It follows, that all the children of men are, 'by nature, children of wrath.' We are all 'guilty before God,' liable to death temporal and eternal.

"And we are all helpless, both with regard to the power and to the guilt of sin. For 'who can bring a clean thing out of an unclean?' None less than the Almighty. Who can raise those that are *dead*, spiritually dead in sin? None but He who raised us from the dust. . . .

"But on what consideration will He do this? 'Not by works of righteousness which we have done.' 'The dead cannot praise Thee, O Lord;' nor do anything for the sake of which they should be raised to life.

"Whatever, therefore, God does, He does it merely for the sake of His well-beloved Son: 'He was wounded for our transgressions, he was bruised for our iniquities.' "

After continuing with a short dissertation on the doctrine of salvation by faith, and the new birth, Wesley said, "You are not ignorant that these are the fundamental doctrines which he everywhere insisted on. And may they not be summed up, as it were, in two words—the new birth, and justification by faith? These let us insist upon with all boldness, at all times, and in all places. . . . Keep close to these good, old, unfashionable doctrines, how many soever contradict and blaspheme."

Wesley ended his discourse with a plea for all to emulate the sweet spirit Whitefield showed to those who disagreed with him and begged his hearers to make allowances for others just as they desired others to do for them. He said, "Then we shall take knowledge of the grace of God which is in every man, whatever be his opinion or mode of worship: then will all that fear God be near and dear unto us 'in the bowels of Jesus Christ.' "

No more appropriate words could have been said at this memorial service than those of Wesley's; they pointed up the ideals to which Whitefield had so successfully and steadfastly given his life and time.

Charles Wesley took up his facile pen and wrote these pensive lines:

"And is my Whitefield enter'd into rest,
With sudden death, with sudden glory blest? . . .

"Can I the memorable day forget,
  When first we, by Divine appointment, met?
  Where undisturb'd the thoughtful student roves,
  In search of truth, through academic groves,
  A modest, pensive youth, who mus'd alone,
  Industrious the frequented path to shun:
  An Israelite without disguise or art,
  I saw, I loved, and clasp'd him to my heart,
  A stranger as my bosom friend carest,
  And unawares receiv'd an angel-guest."

The "prince of preachers" was only 55 years old when he died, but during the years of his ministry he preached 18,000 sermons and wrote 1,460 letters.

Toplady, author of the incomparable hymn "Rock of Ages," said this of Whitefield. "England has had the honor of producing the greatest men, in almost every walk of useful knowledge. At the head of these are: first, Archbishop Bradwardine, the prince of divines; second, Milton, the prince of poets; third, Sir Isaac Newton, the prince of philosophers; and fourth, Whitefield, the prince of preachers."

Sayings of George Whitefield

We must be despised before we can be vessels fit for God's use.

How much comfort do those lose who converse with none but such as are of their own communion!

The reason why congregations have been so dead is because they have had dead men preaching to them.

The farther we go in the spiritual life, the more cool and rational shall we be, and yet more truly zealous.

Learning without piety will only make you more capable of promoting the kingdom of Satan.

Let us be faithful today, and our Lord will support us tomorrow.

I am never so much in my element as when I preach free grace to the chief of sinners.

Vile and unfaithful as I am, my Master lets me have my hands full of work. From morning till midnight, I am employed; and I am carried through the duties of each day with almost uninterrupted tranquillity.

The company of the Son of man is never so sweet as when He walks with us in the fiery furnace.

Of all disputants, religious disputants are the most obstinate and fiery.

If the devil can persuade us not to resist, but to commune with him, he has gained a great point.

Secure sinners must hear the thundering of Mount

Sinai, before we bring them to Mount Zion. They who never preach up the law, it is to be feared, are unskillful in delivering the glad tidings of the gospel. Every minister should be a Boanerges, a son of thunder, as well as a Barnabas, a son of consolation.

Tertullian compares the church in his time to a mowed field; the more frequently it is cut, the more it grows.

Those who are to be highly exalted, must first be deeply humbled.

If riches leave not the owner, the owner must soon leave them.

Religion never prospers when it has too much sunshine.

We are immortal till our work is done.

I always observed, as my inward strength increased, so my outward sphere of action increased proportionably.

Every day and every hour must we be passing from death to life. Mortification and vivification make up the whole of the divine work in the newborn soul.

Christ is the believer's *hollow square;* and if we keep close in that, we are impregnable. Here only I find my refuge. Garrisoned in this, I can bid defiance to men and devils.

All are not possessors that are professors.

Lay in a good stock for your children, get a good many prayers in for them; they may be answered when you are dead and gone.

Would ministers preach for eternity, they would act the part of true Christian orators, for then they would endeavour to move the affections and warm the heart, and not constrain their hearers to suspect that they dealt in the false commerce of unfelt truth.